ARE THEY CRAZY?

THE ULTIMATE GUIDE TO THE CANDIDATE FOR AMERICA'S NEXT PRESIDENT

Prof. Barry A. Goodfield, Ph.D., DABFM

Printed in the United States of America
First Printing: August 2015

ISBN 978-0-9969899-0-9

Cover by John Allen

DEDICATION

This book and our way of life could not exist if we did not have "fools" like the 26 people who were willing to toss their hats in the ring to help make a great country even better. Now that is courage!

CONTENTS

CONTENTS

CONTENTS

CONTENTS

CONTENTS

ACKNOWLEDGMENTS

Special thanks for the fantastic editors Dori Goodfield and Kay Norman, who invested countless hours insuring truth and accuracy by checking and rechecking facts, and to John Allen for his creative cover design.

PREFACE

Why would anyone be crazy enough to run for president?

This book is a look into the unconscious mind and deep-driving forces of both Republican and Democratic candidates wanting to be our next president. This is an intimate profile, an exploration, into the thoughts and feelings of the soon-to-be most powerful person on the planet — the president of United States.

The 2011 edition of *So You Want To Be My President? The Ultimate Voters' guide*, predicted many of the actions that have been taken by President Obama. *"His self-concept is that of a person who is capable of negotiating the nonnegotiable. His early history in Chicago and later in his early political career supports this psychological database. He is a seasoned opponent with a silver tongue."*

The questions are perhaps even more important in 2016. What can we know about the candidates' unconscious motivations? What can we see? Most important, what can we expect? These are the questions that are addressed and explored in *Are They Crazy?*

I will probe all the candidates where presumed to be running for the White House with the same analytical tools utilized at NATO headquarters in Brussels and the International Criminal Tribunal in The Hague. I hope this will help you when you go to the voting booth.

President Franklin D. Roosevelt made two remarks that are relevant to this book. *"Democracy cannot succeed unless those who express their choice are prepared to choose wisely. The real safeguard of democracy, therefore, is education."* He also said, *"Presidents are selected, not elected."*

It is my profound hope that this book will help in your selection.

Barry Austin Goodfield, Ph.D.
August 2015

CHAPTER 1

WHY WOULD ANYBODY WANT TO BE PRESIDENT?

As a profiler, psychologist and psychotherapist, I've profiled virtually every type of individual — from crooks to crown princes from prime ministers to pedophiles. For the last election cycle, I even wrote a book about it, *So You Want To Be My President? The Ultimate Voters Guide, Volume 1.*

I got asked the same question regularly: "What kind of people in this crazy world would want to be president?" I asked this question to my 17-year-old daughter Jane Felice, who seemingly knows everything. "That's easy, Dad." she said. "They want to have power. They think they've got what it takes to do the job." Oh, I thought, like a 17-year-old.

Alejandro, or Alo for short, our bright 19-year-old neighbor added, "They don't like the job that the last president did, and think they can do better." Smart stuff, I thought. "The world is a mess, and I'm the person who has a plan to fix it."

Next comes the MTV pitch: We need three things to win. We all know MTV, but in this case it stands for Money, Trust and Vote — not necessarily in that order.

Not completely satisfied with those answers, as they seemed so simple, I went to my wife Dori. She told me without hesitation, "It's ego, and a belief that they can do some good in the world."

For the last months, I've been in the brains and hearts — and I've even speculated about the role of other organs — in the monumental decision to run for the presidency.

Power and the presidency

I thought of what Abraham Lincoln said: "Nearly all men can stand adversity; but if you want to test a man's character, give him power."

The application or would-be application of power is always part of the presidential discussion. Surely this was a constant comment on the part of debating opponents. Values, morals, patriotism, ethics and even intelligence are the fodder of those who would lead our country. It seems that the taller you sit in the saddle (that is, have name recognition and public attention),

1

the greater the chance that the rest of the would-be presidential pack is likely to try to impugn your character. That is an attempt to bring you down in the polls so they can replace you, and then others will do the same to them.

It is simply, on some level, a sport that happens every two or four years for those who would guide our country. Perhaps the real truth is that those holding public office are constantly campaigning for re-election. But what about what Lincoln said? All of those who run for president have some level of recognition and some power. So why should seeking the presidency bring out all this vitriolic behavior?

The one-word answer is *power*; the two-word answer is *more power*. The operational thinking seems to be, "When you go down, I'll go up." This is alternative thinking, namely, "I'm a better alternative than you! Whenever I can do something that will cast aspersions on the character of others running for the presidency, it may very well boost me in the polls."

Negative campaign advertising

Few candidates endorse this policy, and even fewer will acknowledge that they use negative campaign advertising because it works! How does this relate to Lincoln's remarks? What do we teach our children? That negativity works? This thought does not suggest that it's a good idea to push the other guy down, so you can get your way and what you want. But somehow, this seems to be the essence of political campaigning today. How can we explain this? Have we evolved into a bunch of narcissistic self-centered people, willing to exploit others for our own benefit? Do we delight in the national squabbling in the public sandbox? It makes good television, of this there is no doubt. It is as if the closer the candidate behaves as if he is a starring guest on the Jerry Springer Show, the greater attention he will get regardless of whether it is good or bad. It simply doesn't make any difference. It is like swimming in a public pool: There are those who try to get attention by making a big splash, and there are those who appreciate attention given to skill, agility and style.

Where is the notion of compassion, understanding and forgiveness in political and public life? Ultimately it's about winning. It seems that some are more concerned with victory than what they must do to achieve it.

George C. Scott's portrayal of General George S. Patton in the movie of the same name comes to mind. When he addressed his troops he said: "Americans love a winner and will not tolerate a loser. The thought of losing is hateful to all Americans." Katy bar the door — we're heading toward November!

Are we building our legacy on clichéd remarks, shallow thinking and simplistic self-serving views of our great country? Of course, on some level it's a matter of how you see things, which may or may not accurately reflect reality. We are able to delude ourselves in our attempt to use and understand power by watching biased news programs that reflect far-left or far-right positions. We come away convinced that we have learned the truth from biased "truth"-sayers, who are able to articulate our fears and fantasies. It is like an echo in a canyon bouncing back — bigger but not with more truth, simply more volume. The mass media has made it possible for us to rejoice and validate ourselves with the thoughts of others.

George R.R. Martin, in his book, A Clash of Kings, said:
"Power resides only where men believe it resides. [...] A shadow on the wall, yet shadows can kill. And often times a very small man can cast a very large shadow."

So it is with the race for the presidency. Illusions and images can cast shadows of a small person made larger by the distorted eye of a television lens.

Scripted debates of people parroting polished positions written by spin doctors, judged by people on presentation and not content — is that what we have come to in our democracy? They bare the same level of truth and validity as one of Donald Trump's beauty pageants.

Beth Revis, wrote in her book *Across the Universe*,
"Power isn't control at all — power is strength, and giving that strength to others. A leader isn't someone who forces others to make him stronger; a leader is someone willing to give his strength to others that they may have the strength to stand on their own."

This philosophical statement is in fact one of the pillars upon which our democracy was built. How is it, then, that this gaggle of wise people, with their individual bias and positions, propose to get beyond their own self-serving thinking? The good news is that our democracy and our presidency, for that matter, is pretty darn strong. It has survived liars, louts, fools and fuzzy thinkers for hundreds of years. There's always one or more groups out of power, with a suspicious eye on those holding the reins.

It's not just the notion of checks and balances. It's the suspicion, distrust and disdain of the guy sitting in the backseat staring at the back of the head of the fool whose hands are on the wheel.

Unconscious factors in the presidential race

To me, the answer boils down to three elements in the unconscious minds of those who would be president. I first wrote about them in my book, *Insight and Action: The Role of the Unconscious from Personal to International Levels*, while a Professor at the Diplomatic Academy of London in the early

1990s.

There they were again, the concepts that describe the formation and power of the unconscious mind — *Powerlessness, Injustice, and Loss.*

To me they are the core motivating factors in the formation of the unconscious personality. It certainly can be useful to deduce the thinking that a candidate might have to become the leader of the free world.

Just as *Powerlessness, Injustice, and Loss* are factors which can explain the development of psychological problems on both conscious and unconscious levels. They can also be looked at as motivating influences, for those seeking power, for the regress of grievances early in life development.

For those who have suffered under the abuse of power by others, and/or have lived under or witnessed the systemic abuse of power, the Reagan philosophy of "peace through strength" is a natural fit. Those remembering the Holocaust and proclaim "never again," are referencing all three — powerlessness, injustice and loss. They vow never to become victims again.

We can look at these three variables with three other concepts, One is *intrapsychic* —that is, how people think about the way they think. Two is *psychophysiological* — that is, how our mind-body relationship impacts our action. And third, *interpersonal.* We can probably understand the goals and motivations of an individual and his relationship to the people around him or her.

This is clearly not to suggest that people entering public service are seeking positions of power and influence because they have some psychological disorder or dysfunction. Not so. But when probing the deeper unconscious motivations behind the complex and sometimes overwhelming tasks that go with positions of influence, and looking at the driving force, price and pain as a consequence, it is often interesting to consider underlying motivations.

For a more detailed discussion of these concepts, please see my book *Insight and Action,* or visit our website at www.goodfieldinstitute.com.

Just as people grow into the presidency, they grow out of the need on some level to hold back what they really feel. Roman emperors declared themselves gods, just as Napoleon Bonaparte declared himself an emperor.

John Emerich Edward Dalberg Acton, first Baron Acton (1834–1902), the historian and moralist, who was otherwise known simply as Lord Acton, expressed this opinion in a letter to Bishop Mandell Creighton in 1887: "Power tends to corrupt, and absolute power corrupts absolutely. Great men are almost always bad men."

Gosh, I thought to myself, nothing seems to have changed. Liberals dislike and don't trust conservatives, and vice versa. It is not above either camp to infer evil intent or malicious motivation on the part of the other.

Depending on the news source you choose for information, it is quite possible to receive a daily stream of reinforcement. The news convinces you that the truth is being whispered into your ear, and what is presented in front of your eyes is correct. I have friends, who swear only by Fox News and I have friends who swear only by CNN. Of course, both of these networks, although denying a bias, clearly have one.

In an attempt for full disclosure I must admit that, as a very early riser, I have the added benefit of being treated to the "real truth." It sounds even more trustworthy and believable when delivered with a proper British accent as it is on the BBC. On occasion, a whole broadcast may go by without even one mention of the colonies. Imagine!

Some could become disheartened when listening to and being bombarded by all the analysis, interpretations, the whys and hows.

Donald Trump and Hillary Clinton are motivated, on some level, by the issue of powerlessness. Just as, Bernie Sanders and Rand Paul might find injustice as a strong motivating factor in their campaigns. Again, this is not to say that this is their primary motivation. It is, however, an acknowledgment of the public persona that leads to this suggestion and conclusion.

Bird feeders, fishing poles and political campaigns are geared toward, drawing certain responses from the chosen population. Fishing with the wrong bait, just as sprinkling the wrong birdseed, will not attract the chosen population. So it is with a bad political campaign — a hollow slogan.

Contenders for the presidential prize pay big bucks for word wizards, spin doctors, prognosticators and diviners. Those professing to have these skills and the magic words hope they will lead to a right hand up and another one on the Bible on January 20, 2017, when the whole world watches the fruits of their success. There is little chance that Mr. Smith will go to Washington. These days, legions of people with skill and precision that would make a Swiss watchmaker jealous and, of course, obscene amounts of money, will do the job.

A little luck doesn't hurt either, such as bad weather or conversely good weather on election day. Or last minute sex scandals about your opponent, or a recent debate when your opponent tripped over words, or even better, a staircase. The discovery of a "love child" is always a plus in the campaign, as long as it's not yours.

Because America does not have a king or queen, we make monarchs out of our presidents. We want them to have movie-star celebrity or, conversely, to have been a movie star. What is clear is that we do not want an ordinary person like we had with Harry Truman or dopes like Warren G. Harding and Calvin Coolidge. We will go for the candidate with straight, white teeth and a crooked smile over a pudgy, short guy with glasses like Teddy Roosevelt. Nixon was known to lament about losing the election to John F. Kennedy because of his television debate performance. Nixon perspired and looked like he needed a shave. That cost him the White House — bad luck for him!

Is it unfair to want to have an attractive, articulate representative of the free world, one who is willing to stand up to the outrage and injustice that daily crosses the desk of the president?

Of course there's nothing wrong with that. It is, however, desirable to have the package contains substantive, high-quality content. It is my hope and intent to offer the reader of this 2015 edition of *Are They Crazy? The Ultimate Guide to the Candidates for America's Next President* just that — a deeper more profound look into the psychological aspects of those who aspire to lead this great nation to even greater successes and a brighter future.

Oh, yeah, one more thing — in answer to the question "Why would anybody want to be president?" I think my dad said it best, "You'd have to have a hole in your head!"

CHAPTER 2

THE GOODFIELD METHOD

A few words about our personality and the 12 Goodfield Personality Types of those who are in the White House as their next domicile.

You can't go through life without personality. Of course, we like some personalities better than others. Over the years I have developed a system that describes the characteristics of twelve basic personality types.

It doesn't take Sigmund Freud or Albert Einstein to realize that, of the 12 personality types I hypothesize, not all 12 are represented by the individuals running for the White House. There is an explanation: Simply put, not all of the dozen personalities would find the presidency an interesting or attractive proposition.

Not everybody would want to have an army of busybodies, pundits and partisan political types poking around in their life today, and every day since they were born. This is not to say that there is not presidential timber in all 12 of the Goodfield Personality Types.

It is also important to note that sanity, good judgment and even mental health are inherent characteristics in all of the personalities. What distinguishes one personality from another is a basic style and approach to dealing with the daily challenges we all face.

Each of the candidates, who has chosen to embark on this grueling path to 1600 Pennsylvania Avenue has his or her own unique styles, strategies and stressors. What is interesting is that there tend to be some similarities and differences in the evaluation of the candidates.

There are some basic assumptions that may be considered in judging the judgments of those who would govern us:

Number 1, the unconscious can be seen. Freud talked about it in 1905 when he said, *"When I set myself the task of bringing to light what human beings keep hidden within them, not by the compelling power of hypnosis, but by observing what they say and what they show, I thought the task was a harder one than it really is. He who has eyes to see and ears to hear may convince himself that no mortal can keep a secret. If his lips are sealed, he chatters with his fingertips; betrayal oozes out of him at every pore, and thus the task of making conscious the most hidden recesses of the mind is one which it is quite possible to accomplish."*

Now with new technologies like video, computer programs and invasive techniques, we can with increasing accuracy see the motivation and unconscious forces operating in us all. In video, slow-motion techniques and still frames reveal our deeper thoughts and driving forces.

We will examine, with all who would be president, those forces and desires that explain their actions and clarify their approaches.

Number 2, with stress goes regression. This fact is clearly illustrated when looking at a properly dressed person, standing by an automobile, kicking a flat tire or conversely blasting the horn while pounding the steering wheel in traffic. These are human reactions. Nevertheless they are regressive pieces of behavior, which harken back to early childhood when as children we threw a fit when wishes and desires were not met. It is normal to act abnormally. We all find times in our life when we want to hang out that window and yelled Paddy Chayefsky words from his 1976 film "Network", *"I'm mad as hell and I'm not going to take it anymore."*

For some the idea of sacrificing their privacy and history for a shot at the White House simply isn't worth it. Some would want to avoid the daily stressful grind and consistent confrontation this road demands. In no way does this signify a character flaw. In fact, it may suggest good judgment.

CHAPTER 3

THE NON-VERBAL LEAK

What is so special about the Non-Verbal Leak (NVL), as I call it?

It is observable, learnable, testable and reflects the other half of our message, a half that we may not even know about ourselves. If we can learn to read and understand these powerful communications from the unconscious recesses of the personality, then a new source of deeper data is revealed. That information can change the way we see ourselves and others. This has implications for the person on the pillow next to you or the dictator across the border.

It is simply a formal introduction to a different language that we have all used our entire lives with varying degrees of success and consequence. We can learn to understand it and use it to our advantage. The NVL is the silent language of the unconscious: silent yet powerful, visible yet often consciously unseen, influential yet often denied. It seduces, sabotages and subjugates us in our daily interactions with others. This book is a look at how it works and how it impacts us on all levels of life.

The Non-Verbal Leak can be learned as well as any other language can be learned. It is the other half of our own language. The NVL is a new yet familiar step into the human communication process. With these new tools many mysteries unravel and are revealed. Why some relationships are doomed from the moment that they started. Why we are masters at snatching failure from the jaws of success. Why we make ourselves sick or insane. When we can see — literally see — the messages from the unconscious, we can truly become the masters of our own destiny.

Being able to more accurately read the messages from the unconscious does not mean that you will magically find success or happiness. It simply means that you will have a deeper understanding of yourself and those around you. That knowledge tends to change life.

The microscope and telescope did not create that which was not there. They simply provided a closer look and that consequently changed the way we saw and lived our lives. The Non-Verbal Leak is simply another life-viewing tool.

Many people profess to possess this skill. Crossed arms mean that someone is hiding something. While sitting a leg moving up and down indicates aggression.

Yes and no. Just as "hasta la vista, baby," may have one meaning when friends wave goodbye at the airport or another when uttered by Arnold Schwarzenegger. Context determines meaning and perception determines reality. The context in which an event takes place provides the framework that is helpful to define the meaning of the event. In a situation where a team is losing badly one might say, "They are being killed." Simply put, we are talking comparatively about what is in relationship versus what is expected. Therefore, context determines meaning and perception determines reality because it reflects the facts as we see them; this does not mean that they capture all of what there is to see.

When we think of nonverbal behavior it is possible to have a very quick reaction that others around may not record on a conscious level, but might record as a feeling "tone" that could affect their translation of the overall message. Just as your own language patterns are unique to you, so it is with your regards to your nonverbal language.

What is a Non-Verbal Leak?

The NVL is a repetitive, patterned movement from the shoulders up, reflecting an unresolved perceived trauma and manifesting an Old Decision or strategy from the past. It is a way of looking at the strategies that the individual presents in his total nonverbal behavior.

DEFINITION OF THE NON-VERBAL LEAK

The Non-Verbal Leak (NVL) is an often extraordinarily rapid, repetitive, patterned series of movements.

- It is from the shoulders up
- It reflects an unresolved Perceived Traumatic Event (PTE)
- It manifests a decision and a strategy from the past
- It is a decision and strategy believed to have been appropriate at the time, but maladaptive here and now
- When we look at an NVL, we are looking at the other half of the message of the body
- The NVL is by definition a double message.

SYMBOLIC LEVEL (SL) OF THE NON-VERBAL LEAK

There are three ways in which the Symbolic Level of the NVL is thought about when evaluating it to a Symbolic Level. By Symbolic Level is meant the level in which a deeper meaning can be ascribed to the actions shown on the observable nonverbal level. It is decoding the behavior in a way that provides a next step to rendering the deeper unconscious meaning shown in the nonverbal level.

- Impact: the person's first recording of a stimulus entering his system.
- Primary emotion: How the person initially would like to respond to a perceived stimulus.
- Coping strategy: The ultimate way in which a person decided to react to a perceived event.

These three distinct elements are simply a way of decoding nonverbal responses into their unconscious symbolic meaning.

THE IMPACT OR SL 1

Any Perceived Traumatic Event (PTE) is real in the eyes of the person who experienced it. This shock to the system can be recorded on both levels of consciousness. Moreover, the PTE has impact on an intra-psychic, psycho-physiological or interpersonal level.

In The Goodfield Method we talk about six possibilities that can be an Impact

(SL 1):

- Shock (eyes large)
- Trance (eyes that are unfocused, white under eyes)
- Fear (tearing)
- Denial (eyes closing and sometimes one eye looking away)
- Disbelief (eyes closing, eyebrows up)
- Pain (tearing, turn away from)

THE PRIMARY EMOTION OR SL 2

This is the first impulse that the person has to the Perceived Traumatic Event (PTE). It is what he really wants to do.

Primary Emotion can be:

- Anger
- Sadness

COPING STRATEGY OR SL 3

This is what the person DOES, it is not what he wants to do. It's the realization for the person that when he gives in to the feelings of what he wants to do, he could make the situation even worse. It's the compromise that works for him at that moment.

With time and similar perceptions of what his world is like, he develops similar strategies for similar situations.

So something happens (SL 1), it's traumatic, and the first reaction (SL 2) to it is to strike out. But when you start thinking about striking out you say to yourself: "Hey, if I do this I'm going to end up in a world of trouble." The goal (SL 3) is to establish balance and to restore homeostasis to the system.

The SL 3 is the person's basic strategy in dealing with those feelings in his life.

A Coping Strategy can be:

- Denial
- Trance
- Anger in/out
- Sadness
- Calculated Emotional Response (CER), Seduction
- Control or distancing using variations of the other six SL 3s

STRUCTURAL READING OF THE NON-VERBAL LEAK

Integrity: Reading the NVL of an individual requires the highest standards of ethical behavior and integrity of the reader. The NVL reader is looking deeply into a person, which can have enormous consequences for the person when it is not properly handled or communicated. This is the cornerstone of The Goodfield Method. The NVL can be read in person, from a video, photo or any other kind of registration.

Reading the NVL is organizing information that is available on the screen. Dividing this screen into four quadrants makes it an easier process. Quadrant 1 and 3 are on the left side of the video or photo and represent the right side of the individual. Quadrant 2 and 4 are the right side of the video and represent the left side of the individual.

The Quadrants

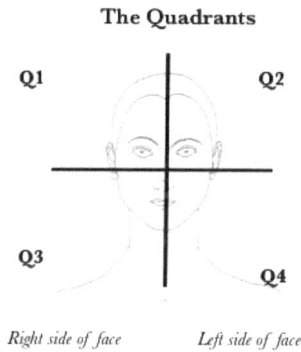

Q1   Q2

Q3   Q4

Right side of face   *Left side of face*

Most people in this world have an unfamiliar feeling when they see themselves on video or on photo. The reason is that the individual sees him/herself in a way other people are used to see them, but the image is just a turnaround from a mirrored image.

This unfamiliar image gives the individual nothing else than an encounter with him/herself. Here we meet the unconscious.

Want to learn the secret psychological underpinnings of candidates running for the U.S. presidency? Learn their unique Non-Verbal Leak!

CHAPTER 4

JOE BIDDEN

OFFICIAL PORTRAIT

"THE INQUISITOR"

A loved politician who shoots from his lip and often misses his target.

BACKGROUND INFORMATION

Current job	Vice President of the United States
Born	November 20, 1942 in Scranton, PA
Religion	Roman Catholic
Family	Jill Jacobs (m. 1977), Neilia Hunter (†) Children: Joseph R. "Beau" (†), Robert Hunter, Naomi Christina (†), Ashley Blazer

PREVIOUS EXPERIENCE

Vice President Biden became an attorney in 1969, and was elected to the New Castle County Council in 1970. He was first elected to the Senate in 1972, the sixth-youngest senator in U.S. history and one of only 18 senators who took office before reaching the age of 31. He was re-elected to the Senate six times, and was the fourth-most-senior senator at the time of his resignation.

Vice President Biden was a long-time member and former chairman of the Foreign Relations Committee. His advocacy helped bring about U.S. military assistance and intervention during the Bosnian War. He opposed the Gulf War in 1991. He voted in favor of the Iraq War Resolution in 2002, but later proposed resolutions to alter U.S. strategy there.

Biden has also served as chairman of the Senate Judiciary Committee, dealing with issues related to drug policy, crime prevention, and civil liberties. He led the legislative efforts for creation of the Violent Crime Control and Law Enforcement Act, and the Violence Against Women Act. He chaired the Judiciary Committee during the contentious U.S. Supreme Court nominations of Robert Bork and Clarence Thomas.

Biden unsuccessfully sought the Democratic presidential nomination in 1988 and 2008, both times dropping out early in the race. President Obama selected Biden to be the Democratic Party nominee for Vice President in the 2008 U.S. presidential election, which they won.

Biden is the first Roman Catholic and the first Delawarean to become Vice President of the United States.

GOODFIELD PERSONALITY TYPING
TYPE 3.2 THE INQUISITOR
I am on my way so get out of my way - please

First Impression

- Outspoken and tough
- Constant state of alert
- A outspoken "scrapper"
- Approachable and bombastic
- Interested in others
- Outwardly open, inwardly closed
- Has the power to hang on
- Humor with irony

Photo Courtesy Political
Ticker CNN

Five reasons why this person is the Inquisitor type 3.2

1. Eyebrow up
2. Shifting of jaws
3. Eyes closing, but not completely (distrust)
4. Difference between left & right side of mouth
5. Blocked breathing

Symbolic Level of Non-Verbal Leak

SL 1 - Pain
SL 2 - Anger
SL 3 - Control by:
- smiling it away
- intellectualization
- swallowing down

PHOTO COURTESY OF GAGE SKIDMORE

Non-Verbal Leak (NVL)

- Eyes open
- Eyes shiny
- Shifting of jaws

- Eyebrow(s) up
- Building up pressure around mouth
- Mouth open
- Showing teeth
- Mouth closed
- Eyes closing, but not completely (distrust)
- Swallow down
- Eyes open

Unconscious Meaning of the NVL
  "I feel pain. It makes me angry. I can't show it, so I keep it inside, swallow it down and look for a hole in others' logic that justifies me to let it out."

PSYCHOLOGICAL OBSERVATION AND PUBLIC COMMENTS

Vice President Joe Biden is a man who is noted for "shooting from the hip with his lip." He is outspoken and tough talking. He's a "scrapper," often finding himself in a scrape because of his statements.

Biden is a lover of people and a fighter for those who suffer injustice. Compassion and approachability exude from every pore. He has suffered great personal loss and tragedy. Somehow it never stops him from doing his duty.

Biden is a "people person" who prides himself on interpersonal contact with the average American. As a senator, most days he rode the train home to Delaware Pennsylvania while getting to know the people with whom he shared the railroad car.

Vice President Biden has always had the power to influence those around him.

He is persuasive and attracted to power. He is a successful leader who is trustworthy, self-assured, and calm in a crisis — which he often finds himself in as a result of his outspoken and sometimes ill-spoken remarks.

Vice President Biden is determined and has the self-concept of a winner. He is more passionate than intelligent, and is not afraid to lead. He is opinionated. He can be explosive and combative when he feels wronged or when the cause for which he is fighting is attacked.

President Obama has not publicly endorsed his Vice President as a logical replacement for him. With the tremendous popularity of Hillary Clinton, it would appear he is holding off judgment. Obama will make his final endorsement if and when he feels the need to do so.

Vice President Biden faces a daunting challenge with the likes of Hillary Clinton, not to mention any potential Republican candidate. It would appear that some individuals do not anticipate a serious attempt at the presidency by Biden.

Although he has a very successful political career and years of experience, some may very well see Biden as a kind of lightweight, who talks too much and needs a muffler on his mouth.

CHAPTER 5

JEB BUSH

PHOTO CROPPED WIKIMEDIA COMMONS

"THE DOER"

A clear-thinking, nice, reasonable, passionless person lacking luster.

BACKGROUND INFORMATION

Current job	Banker, consultant
Born	February 11,1953 in Midland,TX
Religion	Episcopalian (before 1995) Roman Catholic (1995 - present)
Family	Columba Garnica Gallo (m. 1974) Children: George, Noelle Lucilia, John Ellis

PREVIOUS EXPERIENCE

John Ellis "Jeb" Bush is an American businessman and politician who served as the 43rd Governor of Florida from 1999 to 2007. He is the second son of former President George H. W. Bush and former First Lady Barbara Bush, and the younger brother of former President George W. Bush.

Bush grew up in Houston, Texas. He earned a degree in Latin American affairs. Following his father's successful run for vice president in 1980, he moved to Florida and pursued a career in real estate development. In 1986, Bush was named Florida's Secretary of Commerce, a position he held until his resignation in 1988 to help his father's successful campaign for the presidency.

In 1994, Bush made his first run for office, narrowly losing the election for governor by less than two percentage points to the incumbent Lawton Chiles. Bush ran again in 1998 and defeated Lieutenant Governor Buddy MacKay with 55 percent of the vote. Governor Bush ran for reelection in 2002 and won with 56 percent to become Florida's first two-term Republican governor. During his eight years as governor, Bush was credited with initiating environmental improvements, such as conservation in the Everglades, supporting caps for medical malpractice litigation, moving Medicaid recipients to private systems, and instituting reforms to the state education system, including the issuance of vouchers and promoting school choice.

GOODFIELD PERSONALITY TYPING
TYPE 2 THE DOER
Boundary Checker

First Impression
- Dignified
- "The guy next door"
- Approachable
- A good judge of character
- Thoughtful and polite
- Determined at times

Photo Courtesy Of Gage Skidmore

Five reasons why this person is the Doer type 2
1. Eyes wide open
2. Very pronounced jaws
3. Tongue out
4. Pressured defiant appearance
5. Tension in shoulders

Symbolic Level of Non-Verbal Leak

SL 1 - Shock/fear

SL 2 - Anger out

SL 3 - Control by:
- acting out
- distrust
- block in jaws
- swallowing down

PHOTO COURTESY OF GAGE SKIDMORE

Non-Verbal Leak (NVL)
- Eyes open
- Eyes wide open
- Pronounced jaws sometimes pulsing
- Tongue out quick
- Tightening of the mouth

- High breathing
- Lines throat deeper
- Concentration lines stronger
- Movement of the shoulders
- Eyes close not completely (one eye more than the other)
- Eyes open

Unconscious Meaning of the NVL
"I feel unnoticed, that makes me angry. I try not to express it, so I swallow those feelings down, smiling it away until they come out later. And they really do!"

PSYCHOLOGICAL OBSERVATION AND PUBLIC COMMENTS

Governor Bush is very clear about the direction in which he wants to go. In that sense he has drive and purpose.

His soft-spoken approach has been inspirational to some and perhaps frustrating to others, as he blazes his own path his own way.

He is active as a Doer. He has a long fuse, but he can be explosive. He is quite capable of re-evaluating and adapting to change.

Governor Bush has a deeper understanding of people and their needs. He is a natural salesman of his views and values, which are strongly rooted in his family background.

He is not a bombastic or flamboyant individual. However, he is a master in the art of influence. He possesses subtle charm and has good contact with those around him. Bush is a good speaker and understands concepts very well. He is persuasive and can focus on needs, goals and objectives easily. In fact he is a dynamo where needs and goals are concerns. He easily inspires others to join him in his efforts. In that sense he is both persuasive and persistent. Action is more of a priority than intimacy.

Bush is a man who stands in a shadow that stretches back for generations. In his own right, he is a natural leader. His campaign for the presidency will be evaluated in relationship to the successes and failures of those who went before him by the name of Bush. There is a psychodynamic that must drive and influence his behavior in this regard.

Bush stands close to his family, but he must be seen as his own man. His name is the good news and the bad news for his candidacy for the presidency.

CHAPTER 6

BEN CARSON

OFFICIAL PHOTO CARSON SCHOLARS FUND

"THE DOUBTER"

Like most surgeons, sometimes wrong but never in doubt.

BACKGROUND INFORMATION

Current job	Author, political pundit
Born	September 18, 1951 in Detroit, MI
Religion	Seventh-day Adventist
Family	Lacena "Candy" Rustin (m. 1975) Children: Murray, Benjamin, Rhoeyce

PREVIOUS EXPERIENCE

Carson is the son of Sonya Copeland and Robert Solomon Carson, a Seventh-day Adventist minister. Both his parents came from rural Georgia. A DNA test on the television series African American Lives stated that he is of 80 percent African and 20 percent European ancestry. His parents divorced when he was eight years old, and he and his ten-year-old brother Curtis were raised by their mother.

In his book *Gifted Hands*, Carson related that in his youth, he had a violent temper. Once, while in the ninth grade, he nearly stabbed a friend during a fight over a radio station, instead breaking the knife blade. After this incident, he began reading the Book of Proverbs, applying verses on anger and thereafter "never had another problem with temper."

Carson attended Southwestern High School in Detroit, where he excelled in JROTC. He quickly rose in rank and was offered an appointment to West Point.

Carson graduated from Yale University, where he majored in psychology. He received his M.D. from the University of Michigan Medical School. He completed his residency in neurosurgery at Johns Hopkins Hospital in Baltimore.

Carson was a professor of neurosurgery, oncology, plastic surgery, and pediatrics, and he was the director of pediatric neurosurgery at Johns Hopkins Hospital.

At age 33, he became the youngest major division director in the hospital's history as director of pediatric neurosurgery. He was also a co-director of the Johns Hopkins Craniofacial Center.

Carson specialized in traumatic brain injuries, brain and spinal cord tumors, achondroplasia, neurological and congenital disorders, craniosynostosis, epilepsy, and trigeminal neuralgia.

Carson has served on the boards of the Kellogg Company, Costco, and the Academy of Achievement. He is an emeritus fellow of the Yale Corporation.

In March 2013, Carson announced he would retire as a surgeon, stating "I'd much rather quit when I'm at the top of my game." His retirement became official on July 1, 2013.

On July 8, 2013, Carson joined The Washington Times as a weekly opinion columnist. He also writes for American CurrentSee, an online publication for conservative African-Americans. Carson has written six bestselling books.

In 2008, Carson was awarded the Presidential Medal of Freedom by President George W. Bush.

Carson joined the Republican Party on November 4, 2014, the day the 2014 midterm elections took place, as "truly a pragmatic move."

GOODFIELD PERSONALITY TYPING
TYPE 3 THE DOUBTER
Searching for the truth with a big "T"

First Impression
- Tough
- Fair
- Prideful
- A fast judge of character
- Once "read" by him, that's it
- Concerned about how he is seen

Photo Courtesy Of Gage Skidmore

Five reasons why this person is the Doubter type 3
1. Eyebrows up
2. Teariness and tightening eyelids (squinting)
3. Somewhat developed jaws
4. Tongue out/in
5. Blocked breathing

Symbolic Level of Non-Verbal Leak

SL 1 - Disbelief/pain

SL 2 - Anger

SL 3 - Control by:
- intellectualization
- calculated emotional response

PHOTO COURTESY OF GAGE SKIDMORE

Non-Verbal Leak (NVL)
- Eyes open
- Eyebrows up
- Eyes closed
- Eyes open
- Teariness and tightening eyelids (squinting)
- Somewhat developed jaws
- Tension upper lip
- Pressing lips
- Blocked breathing
- Tongue out/in

Unconscious Meaning of the NVL
"I am in pain. I don't believe what happened to me. I am angry and sad. I'm not authorized to express it, so I control it by holding in and intellectualize the feelings."

PSYCHOLOGICAL OBSERVATION AND PUBLIC COMMENTS

Dr. Carson is tough, fair, clearly bright and powerful, with a strong and on some level rigid ego. He is a modest and a quiet force to be reckoned with.

Dr. Carson is orderly and has high expectations of himself and others. He therefore gets quite frustrated when other people don't live up to those expectations.

As a very hard worker, Dr. Carson looks for balance in his life between work and home. Home and family are high priorities for him. His troubled childhood and betrayal by his father (being married and having two families at the same time) have done two things to him: one, to be very protective and loving of his family; two, to become judgmental of those who do not hold the traditional family values he holds so dear.

Dr. Carson still remains reluctant on some level to discuss his true and intimate feelings. Intimacy is always a question with someone with this kind of background. Self-doubt and the fear of rejection certainly drove him hard to achieve the extraordinary successes that he has managed to have by this point in life.

He has historically been in leadership positions where skills and strong intellectual talents are present. He is low-keyed and yet quite a charismatic figure. He has always felt a pressure to succeed at whatever he set as his objectives. He can be passive or outright orally aggressive, which looks less violent but can be very destructive.

All behavior is motivated. A key motivator for Dr. Carson is an unconscious fear of failure and a need to succeed. Without a doubt, he has a great capacity for leadership. At the same time, he is a perfectionist. Like many surgeons, his skill focus and great attention to detail have taken him to the heights of his career. The classic surgeon's remark is, "I'm sometimes wrong but never unsure."

Dr. Carson has the ability to forestall immediate gratification, or put off a reward now, for something more important later. He is regularly admired but on some levels infrequently understood, as he is very complex. The paradox is that he looks as if he is very simple in his actions and goals, but there are very deep motivating factors in his life.

Dr. Carson's self-concept is to do his duty and display good behavior. He is extremely loyal with people that he trusts. If someone criticizes him, he feels attacked, which makes him insecure. He likes to belong to a group; that gives him a secure feeling. He is provocative and passive-aggressive in an intellectualized way. He uses his very high intelligence as a tool to mask his insecurity when he feels attacked or misunderstood.

Dr. Carson can be seen as sympathetic and seeking to meet approval. He is extremely opinionated, and many of his opinions appear to be correct and appreciated by his medical colleagues. His favorite style of leadership is the team player. He places the well being of his team before his own interests; of course, it goes without saying that he is the captain! He is the surgeon! He may be sometimes wrong but *never* in doubt.

As a pediatric surgeon, he is skilled in "fixing" the physical and ultimately psychological problems of children. In some ways he is reaching back into his own childhood with love, compassion and skill to reduce his own pain of himself as a child. What is more, he does it very, very well as he helps many lives!

Dr. Carson is soft-spoken and absolutely fearless when he engages in debate. He is sure of his answers. He is analytical and thinks out the issues about which he has strong feelings. He is compassionate and has deduced strategies and approaches that he feels can and will address the problems from which others suffer. He readily communicates these insights and ideas to others regardless of how provocative they may sound. In fact, the more shocking his observations, the more it pleases him on a deep, unconscious level. "See what I can see. See what I can do!"

Although he is strong with his belief systems and incredibly articulate with regarding his visions of what America needs, he faces strong opposition. Politics is not an arena for nice people trying to do the "right thing."

All those skilled at university politics find it very different from a national campaign to be leader of the free world. There was a book title I remember from years ago; it sums up his situation, *"There Are Men Too Gentle to Live Among Wolves"* by James Kavanaugh.

CHAPTER 7

LINCOLN CHAFEE

PHOTO OF WIKIMEDIA COMMONS

"THE DETERMINATOR"

An independent thinker, whose thinking is sometimes doubtful.

BACKGROUND INFORMATION

Current job	Former Governor of Rhode Island
Born	March 26, 1953 in Providence, RI
Religion	Episcopalian
Family	Stephanie Birney Danforth (m. 1990) Children: Louisa, Caleb, and Thea

PREVIOUS EXPERIENCE

Lincoln Chafee is the son of Republican politician John Chafee, who served as the 66th Governor of Rhode Island (1963–1969), the United States Secretary of the Navy (1969–1972) and a U.S. Senator (1976–1999). Chafee was educated at Providence Country Day School and Phillips Academy, before graduating with a degree in Classics from Brown University. He then moved to Bozeman, Montana, studying to become a farrier at Montana State University, then working at harness racetracks in the United States and Canada.

Chafee returned to Rhode Island and entered politics as a Republican in 1985 as a delegate to the Rhode Island Constitutional Convention. A year later, he was elected to the Warwick City Council, where he served until his election as Warwick's mayor in 1992. When his father died in 1999, Governor Lincoln Almond appointed the younger Chafee to his father's seat in the U.S. Senate. He won the 2000 election to a full term, defeating Democrat Robert Weygand by 57 percent to 41 percent. Chafee left office in January 2007 and then left the Republican Party to become an Independent in September of that year.

Chafee ran for Governor of Rhode Island in the 2010 election becoming the first Independent to serve as Governor of Rhode Island since John Collins in 1790. Governor Chafee was the only Republican in the Senate to vote against authorization of the use of force in Iraq. On June 22, 2006, he was the only Republican to vote for the Levin amendment calling for a non-binding timetable for a withdrawal of U.S. troops from Iraq.

In May 2013, Chafee announced he was switching his registration to the Democratic Party. Until 2015 he was the 74th Governor of Rhode Island.

GOODFIELD PERSONALITY TYPING
TYPE 3.0 THE DETERMINATOR
I will fight for the truth outside of myself

First Impression
- Very strange person
- Major tears in his eyes
- Bizarre thought process
- Big heart, poor focus
- A kind of a "savior" mentality
- A man with something to prove

Photo by K.C. Kzirkel
Wikimedia Commons

Five reasons why this person is the Determinator type 3.0
1. Eyebrows elevated
2. Asymmetrical jaw
3. Teary eyes
4. Concentration line
5. Lines bi-lateral sides of the face

Non-Verbal Leak (NVL)
- Eyes open
- Eyebrows lifted
- Teariness
- Eyes larger
- Eyes Closed

- Eyes open
- Developed jaws a-symmetric
- Biting on self
- Pressure on lips
- Swallowing down
- Eyes open

Unconscious Meaning of the NVL

"I don't believe what happened to me. I am angry and sad about it. I turn those feelings inward and I deny them. Instead I smile, intellectualize and swallow down the feelings."

PSYCHOLOGICAL OBSERVATION AND PUBLIC COMMENTS

Governor Chafee is a pleasant individual. His tentativeness gives the feeling that intimacy may be transitory and elusive for this presidential candidate. He appears somewhat introspective however, even with all the bold moves politically (changing parties), his actions reflect self-doubt and a fear of rejection.

He seeks a simpler but better life for his constituents. In that sense he is idealistic. He continues to get elected; therefore, there must be a base where his views resonate. Chafee is a confusing figure to some as he tries to improve his state. One can argue that he thinks outside the box. Some would argue they don't see any box when they look at him. He is a person of integrity who fights for his constituents. He is not a quitter in hard times.

Chafee's political shifts over the years reinforce the notion of a person looking for something and not finding it. He is certainly his own man! Chafee is an independent thinker to the point we're some might question his thinking. He is clearly bright and willing to consider all options in his role in the politics of Rhode Island.

Chafee's nonverbal behavior shows a lot of pain. It is most clearly seen in his eyes. Below that pain is the level of panic. About what it is not clear. What is clear is that he poses little or no threat to the juggernaut campaign of Hillary Clinton. It is only a question of how he wants to handle his futile attempt at the White House.

Chafee has a history in Rhode Island. He probably will be recorded in its history not as a man who couldn't make up his mind, but as a person more like San Francisco's Emperor Norton — that of a serious political figure representing the great state of Rhode Island.

Governor Chafee takes himself very seriously, believes what he says, and has no hesitation making provocative remarks. Chafee is a modern-day Don Quixote who could benefit from a GPS system.

Chafee is the only Determinator type 3.0 running for President in 2016.

CHAPTER 8

CHRIS CHRISTIE

PHOTO BY MICHAEL VADON WIKIPEDIA COMMONS

"THE INQUISITOR"

A scrapping Jersey boy ready to fight his way to the White House.

BACKGROUND INFORMATION

Current job	Governor of New Jersey
Born	September 6, 1962 in Newark, N.J
Religion	Roman Catholic
Family	Mary Pat (m. 1986)
	Children: Andrew, Sarah, Patrick and Bridget

PREVIOUS EXPERIENCE

Christie is the son of Sondra A. (née Grasso) and Wilbur James "Bill" Christie, a certified public accountant. His father is of German, Scottish, and Irish descent, and his mother was of Sicilian ancestry. At Livingston High School, Christie served as class president and played catcher for the baseball team. Christie's father and mother were Republican and Democratic, respectively.

However, he has credited his Democratic-leaning mother for indirectly making him a Republican by encouraging him in 1977 to volunteer for gubernatorial candidate Tom Kean, who became his role model.

Christie graduated from the University of Delaware with a Bachelor of Arts in political science in 1984 and Seton Hall University School of Law with a J.D. in 1987. Christie was admitted to the New Jersey State Bar Association and the Bar of the United States District Court, District of New Jersey, in December 1987. Later in life, he was awarded honorary doctorate degrees by Rutgers University and Monmouth University.

Christie joined a Cranford, New Jersey, law firm in 1987, rose to become a partner in 1993, and continued practicing until 2002. He was elected county legislator in Morris County, serving from 1995 to 1998, during which time he generally pushed for lower taxes and lower spending. From 2002 to 2008, he was appointed as United States Attorney for New Jersey. In that position, he emphasized prosecutions of political corruption and also obtained convictions for sexual slavery, arms trafficking, racketeering by gangs, and other federal crimes.

From January 2009 until now, Christie has been the 55th Governor of New Jersey.

Christie was seen as a potential candidate in the 2012 presidential election, he was the keynote speaker at the 2012 Republican National Convention. Following the controversial closure of toll plaza access lanes in

Fort Lee in 2013, an internal investigation commissioned by the Governor's Office found no evidence of Christie having prior knowledge of or having directed the closure. During a May 1, 2015 news conference, U.S. Attorney Paul J. Fishman stated that, based upon the then-available evidence, his office would not bring further charges in the case.

GOODFIELD PERSONALITY TYPING
TYPE 3.2 THE INQUISITOR
I am on my way so get out of my way - please

First Impression
- Outspoken and tough
- Constant state of alert
- A outspoken "scrapper"
- Approachable and bombastic
- Interested in others
- Outwardly open, inwardly closed
- Has the power to hang on
- Humor with irony

Photo Courtesy Of Gage Skidmore

Five reasons why this person is the Inquisitor type 3.2
1. Eyebrow up
2. Shifting of jaws
3. Eyes closing, but not completely (distrust)
4. Difference between left & right side of mouth
5. Blocked breathing

Symbolic Level of Non-Verbal Leak

SL 1 - Pain/fear

SL 2 - Anger out

SL 3 - Control by:
- cynicism
- swallowing down
- calculated emotional response

PHOTO COURTESY OF GAGE SKIDMORE

Non-Verbal Leak (NVL)

- Eyes open
- Eyes shiny
- Shifting of jaws
- Eyebrow(s) up
- Building up pressure around mouth
- Mouth open
- Showing teeth
- Mouth closed
- Eyes closing, but not completely (distrust)
- Swallow down
- Eyes open

Unconscious Meaning of the NVL

"*I feel pain and fear, and become angry. My question is: "Shall I show this … or distance myself?*"

PSYCHOLOGICAL OBSERVATION AND PUBLIC COMMENTS

Governor Christie is the "Rocky Balboa" in the 2016 presidential election. He is a "scrapper" who prides himself in his ability to fight for what he believes. He is a "people person," one who is dedicated to helping the people of New Jersey. His bombastic approach is part of his image. He is not a quitter and sees himself as a defender of the underdog. Christie has humor with irony and a quick wit as well.

Governor Christie is a natural salesman and controversial at the same time. He is bright and persuasive, attracted to power and influence. This is the quintessential leader — self-assured, calm in crisis, in fact he revels in conflict and is confident that his perception of the facts is the undeniable truth itself. Christie has a history of risk taking and often a series of successes that validate the decisions behind the risks taken. Add intelligence and education to the Inquisitor and the sky is the limit.

Governor Christie is self-assured and revels in controversy. He is trustworthy and radiates that to those around him. What you see is what you get when dealing with Christie. He has an explosive temper. Add arrogance, strength and determination to that and you have the Governor of New Jersey.

Christie's bombastic approach endears him to some and alienates him from others. This has not been a difficulty in the past; however, in a presidential race he may generate more heat than light. His relentless search for the truth, and his style of achieving the truth, may prove to be too much for those looking for calm, steady leadership in these difficult national and international times.

Christie is a down-home (in a New Jersey-kind of way) guy next door. He is in a regular struggle to get out his position. Constantly on the move, he is a "rebel without a pause." That is both the good and bad news about him. If the American voter is looking for a no-nonsense leader in the White House, Governor Christie may be just the person. However, if negotiation, arbitration and communication are key factors for the voter, his style might be a bit overwhelming. Do not expect any change in approach from this two-fisted fighter.

CHAPTER 9

HILLARY CLINTON

PHOTO COURTESY OF GAGE SKIDMORE

"THE POUNCER"

A person who's been around for years still yelling "I'm new!"

BACKGROUND INFORMATION

Current job	Public speaker
Born	October 27, 1947 in Chicago, IL
Religion	Methodist (United Methodist Church)
Family	Bill Clinton (m. 1975) Child: Chelsea

PREVIOUS EXPERIENCE

Hillary Diane Rodham Clinton's father, Hugh Ellsworth Rodham, was of Welsh and English descent; he managed a successful small business in the textile industry. Her mother, Dorothy Emma Howell, was a homemaker of English, Scottish, French, and Welsh descent. Raised in a politically conservative household, Rodham's early political development was shaped most by her high school history teacher (like her father, a fervent anticommunist who introduced her to Goldwater's The Conscience of a Conservative), and by her Methodist youth minister (like her mother, concerned with issues of social justice and with whom she met civil rights leader Martin Luther King, Jr. in Chicago in 1962).

Hillary Rodham was the first student commencement speaker at Wellesley College in 1969, and she earned a J.D. from Yale Law School in 1973. In 1974 she was a member of the impeachment inquiry staff in Washington, D.C., advising the House Committee on the Judiciary during the Watergate scandal. Rodham helped research procedures of impeachment and the historical grounds and standards for impeachment. The committee's work culminated in the resignation of President Richard Nixon in August 1974. By then, Rodham was viewed as someone with a bright political future — she had the potential to become a future senator or U.S. President.

In 1975 she married Bill Clinton. She co-founded Arkansas Advocates for Children and Families in 1977. She became the first female chair of the Legal Services Corporation 1978 and the first female full partner at Rose Law Firm in 1979.

From 1983 until 1992, Hillary Clinton was the First Lady of Arkansas. From 1993 until 2001, she was First Lady of the United States. Her major initiative, the Clinton health care plan of 1993, failed to gain approval from the U.S. Congress. Her years as First Lady drew a polarized response from the American public. The only First Lady to have been subpoenaed, she testified before a federal grand jury in 1996 regarding the Whitewater controversy, but was never charged with wrongdoing in this or several other investigations during her husband's presidency.

Her marriage to the President was subjected to considerable public discussion following the Lewinsky scandal of 1998. Clinton was elected in 2000 as the first female senator from the state; she is the only First Lady ever to have run for public office. Following the September 11th attacks, she supported military action in Afghanistan and the Iraq Resolution, but subsequently objected to the George W. Bush administration's conduct of the Iraq War. She opposed most of Bush's domestic policies. Clinton was re-elected to the Senate in 2006. Running in the Democratic primaries in the 2008 presidential election, Clinton's campaign won far more primaries and delegates than any other female candidate in American history, but she narrowly lost the nomination to Barack Obama.

As Secretary of State in the Obama administration from January 2009 to February 2013, Clinton was at the forefront of the U.S. response to the Arab Spring and advocated the U.S. military intervention in Libya. She took responsibility for security lapses related to the 2012 Benghazi attack, which resulted in the deaths of American consulate personnel, but defended her personal actions in regard to the matter. Clinton visited more countries than any other Secretary of State. Leaving office at the end of Obama's first term, she authored her fifth book and undertook speaking engagements before announcing her second run for the Democratic nomination in the 2016 presidential election.

GOODFIELD PERSONALITY TYPING
TYPE 2.3 THE POUNCER
Danger on two feet

First Impression
- Strong and powerful
- Very bright
- Focused
- Street smart
- Worldly
- Charming

Official photo as US. Senator

Five reasons why this person is the Pouncer type 2.3
1. Shock showing somewhat in eyes
2. Shifting of jaws
3. Tight top lip
4. Eyebrows pulled together (furrowed)
5. Block in throat

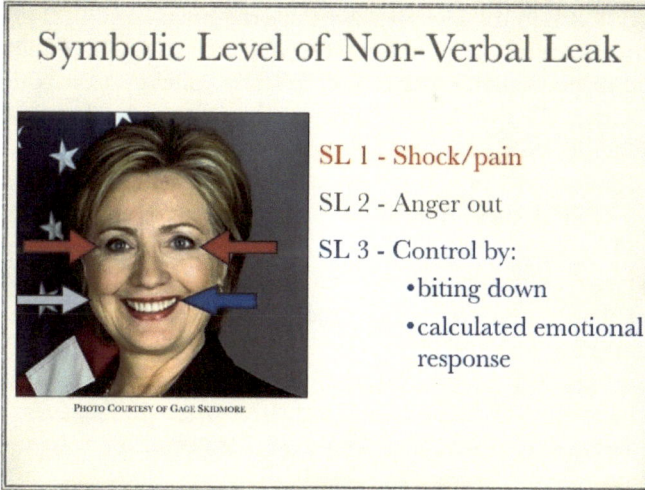

Symbolic Level of Non-Verbal Leak

SL 1 - Shock/pain

SL 2 - Anger out

SL 3 - Control by:
- biting down
- calculated emotional response

PHOTO COURTESY OF GAGE SKIDMORE

Non-Verbal Leak (NVL)
- Eyes open
- Eyes wide open
- Eyes close (may not completely close)
- Masseter muscle pulsing and/or tongue out
- Tighten top lip
- Swallow down
- Eyes open

Unconscious Meaning of the NVL
"I am shocked, and want to express my anger. Instead I hold it inside until I can find the correct opportunity to express it fully."

PSYCHOLOGICAL OBSERVATION AND PUBLIC COMMENTS

Former Secretary of State Hillary Rodham Clinton is likely one of the brightest people running for the presidency in 2016, (with the possible exception being Dr. Carson). She is certainly one with more political baggage than anybody else. Clinton is strong, powerful, driven and focused regarding her objectives. She is well-educated, street-smart and worldly. She has had personal contact with most world leaders with whom she would have to work if elected. Many see her endorsement by the Democratic party as a foregone conclusion, a thought that curls the toes in the boots of many Republicans. Former Secretary of State Clinton is the most powerful person running for the presidency. She is often found at the center of the fray when action is required on a national or international level.

Clinton is a relentless fighter for her objectives; moreover, she is quite experienced at managing a crisis. She skillfully watches a crisis unfold and then takes action. To the chagrin of many, she will present her thoughts and solutions whether they are wanted or not.

When Clinton sets her mind to something, she will devote her full energy to achieve her objectives. Her years of experience on the international scene and her difficulties in her domestic life with husband Bill have shown what strengths and weaknesses she has. Her lifestyle and name recognition make any cause a potential cause célèbre for former Secretary of State Clinton.

The good and bad news is basically the same, if Clinton believes in you or your cause, she will dogmatically fight for what she believes. Although she has superior intelligence, her tactics are often rigid and miss the nuances expressed in divergent opinions.

Clinton is perhaps the most powerful off the 12 Goodfield Personality Types. This is not to say that is how she is seen. It is a clear representation of what she really feels. She is a pressured person. When she feels anger she may show it, or she may repress the impulse and wait for another time and place. This behavior is a partial explanation of the use of Calculated Emotional Response (CER). The other explanation for the use of CER is her distrust and reluctance to act impulsively, lest she derail her course of action in reaching her objective. What is sure is that she will neither forgive nor forget.

Clinton presents a strong well-developed knowledgeable image often seen as confident, sometimes too confident. She may be perceived as arrogant and sometimes aloof. Clinton can be verbally cutting and witty in her expression of her basic aggressive impulses. Like an Abrams tank, she has a tough exterior. When combat is necessary, she battens down the hatches and tunes out conflicting noise and feedback around her. This tactic could win a battle but lose the war.

Former Secretary of State Clinton is without doubt one of the most qualified persons to seek the White House in this election cycle. She is, however, quite a polarizing personality. Her pragmatic attitude and liberal philosophy, as it is with many candidates, allows a kind of myopathy that propels her forward, regardless of the negative response she received in the media.

To the extent that she was a confidant of President Bill Clinton, and perhaps even a "kingmaker," the prospect of a sitting and former president under one roof is either an exciting or horrifying prospect, depending on one's political persuasions.

For America it is an interesting time in history — one that some feel we might not survive. Late night TV hosts and standup comedians are offering up thanksgiving prayers at the thought of such material!

CHAPTER 10

TED CRUZ

OFFICIAL PORTRAIT

"THE INQUISITOR"

A "devoted divider" more interested in his views than in uniting principles.

BACKGROUND INFORMATION

Current job	U.S. Senator from Texas
Born	December 22, 1970 in Calgary, AB
Religion	Southern Baptist
Family	Heidi Nelson (m. 2001) Children: Caroline and Catherine

PREVIOUS EXPERIENCE

Senator Cruz is the son of Eleanor Elizabeth Darragh Wilson and Rafael Bienvenido Cruz. At the time of his birth, Cruz's parents were working in the oil business as owners of a seismic-data processing firm for oil drilling.

Cruz's ancestry is Spanish on his father's side and Irish and Italian on his mother's side. His father left Cuba in 1957 to attend the University of Texas at Austin, and became a naturalized U.S. citizen in 2005. His mother earned an undergraduate degree in mathematics from Rice University in the 1950s.

Cruz graduated cum laude from Princeton University with a Bachelor of Arts in Public Policy from the Woodrow Wilson School of Public and International Affairs in 1992. While at Princeton, he competed for the American Whig-Cliosophic Society's Debate Panel and won the top speaker award at both the 1992 U.S. National Debating Championship and the 1992 North American Debating Championship. In 1992, he was named U.S. National Speaker of the Year, as well as Team of the Year with his debate partner, David Panton. Cruz and Panton represented Harvard Law School at the 1995 World Debating Championship, making it to the semi-finals, where they lost to a team from Australia. Princeton's debate team later named their annual novice championship after Cruz.

After graduating from Princeton, Cruz attended Harvard Law School, graduating magna cum laude in 1995 with a J.D. degree.

Between 1999 and 2003, Cruz was the director of the Office of Policy Planning at the Federal Trade Commission, an associate deputy attorney general at the United States Department of Justice, and domestic policy advisor to U.S. President George W. Bush in the 2000 Bush-Cheney campaign. He served as Solicitor General of Texas from 2003 to May 2008. He was the first Hispanic, the youngest, and the longest-serving solicitor general in Texas history. Cruz was also an adjunct professor of law at the University of Texas School of Law in Austin from 2004 to 2009. While there, he taught U.S. Supreme Court litigation. Cruz is one of three senators of Cuban descent.

Cruz was the Republican nominee for the Senate seat vacated by fellow Republican Kay Bailey Hutchison. Cruz openly identifies with the Tea Party movement and has been endorsed by the Republican Liberty Caucus. Cruz was elected senator in 2012 and is the first Hispanic or Cuban American to serve as a U.S. Senator representing Texas.

GOODFIELD PERSONALITY TYPING
TYPE 3.2 THE INQUISITOR
I am on my way so get out of my way - please

First Impression

- Outspoken and tough
- Constant state of alert
- A outspoken "scrapper"
- Approachable and bombastic
- Two-valued orientation
- Outwardly open, inwardly closed
- Has the power to hang on
- Not open to difference

Photo Courtesy of Gage Skidmore

Five reasons why this person is the Inquisitor type 3.2
1. One eyebrow up
2. Shifting of jaws (smoking behavior)
3. Eyes closing, but not completely (distrust)
4. Difference between left and right side of mouth
5. Blocked breathing

Non-Verbal Leak (NVL)
- Eyes open
- Eyes shiny
- Shifting of jaws
- Eyebrow(s) up
- Building up pressure around mouth
- Mouth open
- Showing teeth
- Mouth closed
- Eyes closing, but not completely (distrust)
- Swallow down
- Eyes open

Unconscious Meaning of the NVL
  "I am in pain and fear, that makes me angry. I don't feel authorized to express it so I swallow it down and control it."

PSYCHOLOGICAL OBSERVATION AND PUBLIC COMMENTS

Senator Cruz is a self-assured, persuasive individual who is attracted to power.

He is a skilled orator and a successful leader. He is trustworthy, calm in a crisis, and comfortable with controversy. Cruz is arrogant and explosive at times, tough and determined to achieve his objectives.

47

Senator Cruz conjures up memories of American politician Joseph McCarthy, who served as a Republican U.S. Senator from the state of Wisconsin from 1947 until his death in 1957. The term McCarthyism, coined in 1950, referred to McCarthy's practices. Today the term is used more generally in reference to demagogic, reckless, and unsubstantiated accusations, as well as public attacks on the character or patriotism of political opponents.

Cruz makes allegations toward his fellow senators that may have some basis in truth. His approach seems to generate more heat than light. At a time when unity and goodwill are necessary, he seems to believe that "divide and conquer" is a superior strategy.

Cruz's strongest support comes from Tea Party supporters who want straight talk, direct action, and no nonsense in between. Although an articulate speaker, Cruz is a polarizing personality who is as interesting and refreshing as is Donald Trump. Both seem to be more expert on what is wrong with America rather than on what is right with America. It is one thing to excite an alienated group of voters, it is quite another to develop and present viable solutions that will be embraced by a larger voting population on a national basis. Perhaps it is time to abandon the "Tea Party's Teapot" and join the "Grand Old Party," if Cruz and his colleagues are serious about the White House in 2016.

CHAPTER 11

BOB EHRLICH

OFFICIAL PORTRAIT

"THE POUNCER"

A bright governor with no name recognition — Bob who??

BACKGROUND INFORMATION

Current job	Attorney
Born	November 25, 1957 in Arbutus, MD
Religion	Methodist
Family	Kendel Sibiski (m.1993) Children: Drew Robert, Joshua Taylor

PREVIOUS EXPERIENCE

Senator Ehrlich is the son of Nancy Bottorf, a legal secretary, and Robert Leroy Ehrlich, a car salesman. He graduated from Princeton University (1979). He continued on to law school, graduating from Wake Forest University School of Law in 1982.

After law school, Ehrlich worked for Ober, Kaler, Grimes and Shriver, a Baltimore law firm, and became active in politics. In 1986, Ehrlich won a seat in the Maryland House of Delegates, representing parts of Baltimore County from 1987 to 1995. He was a moderate Republican representing a Democratic stronghold.

In 1993, 2nd district Representative Helen Delich Bentley announced she would be vacating her seat in the U.S. House of Representatives. Ehrlich announced his candidacy in November and won the election. During his term, he introduced legislation aimed at helping disabled people maintain employment, and supported harsher gun violence penalties.

While in Congress, Ehrlich served on the U.S. House Energy and Commerce Committee. He was also a member of the subcommittees on health, telecommunications and the Internet, and environment and hazardous materials; the Congressional Biotechnology Caucus, where he served as co-chairman; and the Congressional Steel Caucus.

From 2003-2007, Ehrlich became the 60th Governor of Maryland. Ehrlich said that fiscal responsibility, education, health and the environment, public safety, and commerce were the "Five Pillars" of his administration. He opposed sales and income tax increases and supported legalization of slot machines to raise revenue.

Under Ehrlich's tenure, Maryland stayed 0.5 percent or more below the national unemployment average. He endorsed the Thornton Plan, which was passed by the Legislature in 2002. In part, this plan would grant extra money to poorer school systems and those in areas with a higher cost of living.

After pushing though the charter school law in Maryland, Ehrlich oversaw the opening of the first public charter school in the state. During his administration, 45 new schools were constructed, and an additional 52 schools were fully renovated. His administration invested record funding in Maryland community colleges as well as public, historically black colleges in the state.

A month after he left public office, Ehrlich and several aides from his administration opened a Baltimore-area office of the law firm Womble, Carlyle Sandridge & Rice. Ehrlich and his wife hosted their own radio show on WBAL-AM Radio every Saturday from 2007 to 2010.

GOODFIELD PERSONALITY TYPING
TYPE 2.3 THE POUNCER
Danger on two feet

First Impression
- Strong and powerful
- Bright
- Focused
- Street smart
- Determined
- Man of the people
- Not ready for primetime

Wikimedia Commons

Five reasons why this person is the Pouncer type 2.3
1. Shock showing somewhat in eyes
2. Shifting of jaws
3. Tight top lip
4. Eyebrows pulled together (furrowed)
5. Block in throat

Symbolic Level of Non-Verbal Leak

SL 1 - Shock/pain

SL 2 - Anger out

SL 3 - Control by:
- biting down
- calculated emotional response

Picture courtesy of Richard Lippenholz

Non-Verbal Leak (NVL)
- Eyes open
- Eyes wide open
- Eyes close (may not completely close)
- Masseter muscle pulsing and/or tongue out
- Tighten top lip
- Swallow down
- Eyes open

Unconscious Meaning of the NVL
   "I am shocked and want to express my anger. Instead I hold it in until I can find the correct opportunity to express it fully."

PSYCHOLOGICAL OBSERVATION AND PUBLIC COMMENTS

Governor Ehrlich has often found himself in the middle of many controversies, there is no doubt about that. As governor, he certainly had many important decisions to make. On a concept level, he had many well-thought-out positions as well as a clear definition of what a leader supposed to be.

Ehrlich is a clear observer and yet has some distance from the events. It is as if he observes conflict and crisis with great interest and good insights, but somehow from behind the glass wall. It is a paradox. It is as if he doesn't try hard enough, or he tries too hard. Whatever it is, Ehrlich has power; he simply doesn't use it in a convincing way. Ehrlich is a professional when it comes to facts.

He has been a critical player in major decisions. Be it on the gridiron at Princeton, in Congress, State legislature, or at the Governor's office, he was pushing hard to find the right decision. He demonstrated his power of persuasion and good logic as well as his dedication to justice and positive change.

The price tag for this is on his face. Ehrlich has extraordinary tension around his top lip. The masseter muscles show all of the attention and aggression he holds inside.

Ehrlich is strong and clear about his views regarding government and other issues.

He has an outstanding organizational ability and is a clear thinker. His formula for what America needs is leadership and a clear sense of direction. Few would argue with these observations. The problem is only one percent of the polled individuals acknowledge him as the best candidate in the large Republican field.

Ehrlich is not a quitter, but his desire to become President of United States with virtually no name recognition makes his efforts unrealistic and questionable. The question is one of the ego. As an obviously bright, educated and practicing attorney, he must be aware of the realities of his circumstance.

Ehrlich's reactions to questions from the general public about his positions on critical issues show some "rough edges." Referring someone to your book can be perceived as an attempt to dodge the question, and cover ignorance. In his case, this is not the issue. It's simply a matter of experience.

Governor Ehrlich is not ready for prime time in all honesty. I doubt he ever will be.

CHAPTER 12

MARK EVERSON

OFFICIAL PORTRAIT

"THE DOER"

A former big-time taxman trying to go straight in Washington.

BACKGROUND INFORMATION

Current job	Vice Chairman of Alliantgroup
Born	September 10, 1954 in New York City, NY
Religion	Unknown
Family	Nanette Rutka (1984-2008) Children: Leonard Bahadur, Emma Pinar, Amrong, Oliver

PREVIOUS EXPERIENCE

Everson's father, Leonard, was an attorney, and his mother, Marjory, was a chemist before becoming a full time homemaker. Mark grew up in Yonkers with his two siblings. He attended boarding school in Exeter, New Hampshire, starting in the ninth grade. Finishing a year early in 1971, he then lived in Africa for the better part of a year. At age seventeen he managed components of an integrated poultry farm in Kitwe, Zambia. First he ran the butchery, next the broiler grow-out operation, and finally the hatchery.

In 1972 Everson returned to the United States and started college. While at Yale, he studied history and ran on the cross country and track teams. Immediately after graduation, Everson joined the accounting firm Arthur Andersen LLP as an auditor in the New York office. He went to night school at the NYU Business School, earning an MS degree in accounting and becoming a CPA.

Mark Everson is the only presidential candidate with both extensive business and federal executive branch experience.

In the private sector, Everson has held both operating and financial positions within companies in the United States, Turkey, France and Zambia. His assignments ranged from plant manager of a unionized beverage can factory to senior financial positions at the world's largest packaging and airline catering companies.

In the Reagan Administration, Everson held foreign policy and law enforcement positions at the US Information Agency and the Department of Justice. At USIA, Everson worked on sensitive public diplomacy projects, including INF deployment and the establishment of Radio Marti. At the DOJ, Attorney General Ed Meese appointed Everson as Deputy Commissioner at the INS, where he supervised all agency operations, including the Border Patrol and inspectors at the ports of entry.

In the second President George W. Bush's Administration, Everson was Deputy Director for Management at OMB and then Commissioner of the IRS, which achieved record service and enforcement results under his leadership. Everson has state government experience as well, having served in the cabinet of Indiana Governor Mitch Daniels. Under Daniels, he ran Indiana's unemployment insurance and job training programs.

As President and Chief Executive Officer of the American Red Cross he was forced to resign after six months by the Board of Governors for having a personal relationship with a married female subordinate.

GOODFIELD PERSONALITY TYPING
TYPE 2 THE DOER
Boundary Checker

First Impression
- A dreamer with a plan
- A pleasant pusher
- Pressured speech
- Witty and quick
- Well-informed true believer
- Has something to proof

Photo Courtesy of Gage Skidmore

Five reasons why this person is a Doer type 2
1. Eyes wide open
2. Very pronounced jaws
3. Tongue out
4. Pressured defiant appearance
5. Tension in shoulders

Symbolic Level of Non-Verbal Leak

SL 1 - Shock/fear

SL 2 - Anger out

SL 3 - Control by:
- holding in
- denial

YouTube clip announcement 2015

Non-Verbal Leak (NVL)
- Eyes open
- Eyes wide open
- Pronounced jaws sometimes pulsing
- Tongue in/out quick
- Tightening of the mouth
- High breathing
- Lines throat deeper
- Concentration lines stronger
- Movement of the shoulders
- Eyes close not completely (one eye more not completely closed)
- Eyes open

Unconscious Meaning of the NVL
"I feel unnoticed, and that makes me angry. I try not to express it, so I swallow those feelings down, until they come out later. And they really do!"

PSYCHOLOGICAL OBSERVATION AND PUBLIC COMMENTS

Everson has great drive, sense of direction and purpose. He is a dynamo, active and even inspirational at times. Sometimes he can even be explosive.

Everson is a hard worker. He has a logical mind and is dedicated to whatever task is at hand. His dedication and persistence have served him well in his work. Intimacy and contact remain somewhat of a problem.

Everson is a theoretical expert on people and their needs. If you listen to him, his skill in the art of influence and charming personality may be convincing. There is a fundamental distrust of those who are too different in character and personality. Everson is facile with words and concepts and is a natural communicator, with the possible exception of his difficulties as Director of the Red Cross. Intimacy and boundary-setting became an issue.

As a tax expert, he is a good manipulator. He is fast, sometimes too fast.

What is clear is that he completely believes his tax advice will resonate with all taxpayers in America. Without any doubt, his logic and charming approach to people will resonate with those who have enough money to worry about the tax man.

Everson presents an image of a knowledgeable person regarding issues and concerns of the middle-class — specifically, taxation reform and reducing government. His appeal to a larger national base may be limited if he is perceived to have a narrow focus on issues.

There is little chance that Mark Everson will spark an interest on a national level. The larger issues facing America, be they international affairs or domestic issues, may limit his appeal to a larger audience. He is, and has been, a valuable person who is dedicated to the welfare of the American people. The White House, although just down the street from the Internal Revenue Service, may prove to be just too great a distance.

CHAPTER 13

CARLY FIORINA

PHOTO COVER BOOK PUBLISHED SENTINEL PENGUIN RANDOM HOUSE

"THE DOER"

A sophisticated powerhouse with outstanding talents and abilities.

BACKGROUND INFORMATION

Current job	Chair non-profit organization Good360 Chair and CEO of Carly Fiorina Enterprises
Born	September 6, 1954 in Austin, TX
Religion	Christian (raised Episcopalian)
Family	Todd Bartlem (m. 1977-1984), Frank Fiorina (m. 1985) (Step) Children Traci, Lori Ann (†)

PREVIOUS EXPERIENCE

Cara (Carly) Carleton Sneed Fiorina is the daughter of Joseph Tyree Sneed III and Madelon Montross Juergens. At the time of her birth, Fiorina's father was a professor at the University of Texas School of Law. She is mainly of English and German ancestry. She has a brother and a sister.

Fiorina attended five different high schools, including one in Ghana. In college, she studied medieval history and philosophy. After trying law school, she bounced from job to job, working as a receptionist, teaching English in Italy, and finally signing on as a sales rep at AT&T at age 25. In the coming years, she would earn an MBA from the University of Maryland and an MS degree from MIT's Sloan School of Management.

Carly Fiorina is a politician, former business executive, and current chairperson of Good360. Starting in 1980, Fiorina rose through the ranks to become an executive at AT&T and its equipment and technology spinoff, Lucent. As chief executive officer of Hewlett-Packard (HP) from 1999 to 2005, she was the first woman to lead one of the top 20 U.S. companies. In 2002, Fiorina undertook the biggest high-tech merger in history with rival computer company Compaq, which made HP the world's largest personal computer manufacturer. HP gained market share following the merger and subsequently laid off 30,000 of its American workers. By the end of 2005, the merged company had more employees worldwide than they had separately before the merger. By February 9, 2005, HP stock had lost more than half of its value, while the overall NASDAQ index had fallen 26 percent owing to turbulence in the tech sector. On that date, Hewlett-Packard's board of directors forced Fiorina to resign as chief executive officer and chairman.

Assessments of Fiorina's business career have varied. During her time at Lucent and Hewlett-Packard, she was named by Fortune Magazine as the most powerful woman in business. Later in the February 7, 2005 issue,

Fortune described her merger plan as "failing" and the prognosis as "doubtful." She has been described as one of the worst tech CEOs of all time, though others have defended her business leadership decisions and viewed the Compaq merger as successful over the long term. After resigning from HP, Fiorina served on the boards of several organizations and as an advisor to Republican John McCain's 2008 presidential campaign. She won a three-way race for the Republican nomination for the United States Senate from California in 2010, but lost the general election to incumbent Democratic Senator Barbara Boxer by 10 points.

GOODFIELD PERSONALITY TYPING
TYPE 2 THE DOER
Boundary Checker

First Impression

- Dignified
- The girl next door
- Approachable
- A good judge of character
- Thoughtful and polite
- Determined at times

Photo Courtesy Of Gage Skidmore

Five reasons why this person is a Doer type 2

1. Eyes wide open
2. Very pronounced jaws
3. Tongue out
4. Pressured defiant appearance
5. Tension in shoulders

Symbolic Level of Non-Verbal Leak

SL 1 - Shock/fear

SL 2 - Anger

SL 3 - Control by:
- holding in
- swallow down
- denial

PHOTO COURTESY OF GAGE SKIDMORE

Non-Verbal Leak (NVL)

- Eyes open
- Eyes wide open
- Pronounced jaws sometimes pulsing
- Tongue in/out quick
- Tightening of the mouth
- High breathing
- Lines throat deeper
- Concentration lines stronger
- Movement of the shoulders
- Eyes close not completely (one eye more than the other)
- Eyes open

Unconscious Meaning of the NVL

"I feel denied, and that makes me angry. I try not to express it, so swallow those feelings down, and smile them away, until they come out later."

PSYCHOLOGICAL OBSERVATION AND PUBLIC COMMENTS

Carly Fiorina is a strong businesswoman who ran one of the largest companies in the world. Once a secretary, her simple communication style and personable approach reveal a well-informed, clear-thinking individual. She knows what she thinks is the right thing to do. She is informed and formidable!

Fiorina is a person with power, drive and focus. She states her conservative opinions clearly and directly; moreover, she involves herself in organizations that support and defend her conservative positions.

On February 20, 2009, Fiorina was diagnosed with breast cancer. She underwent a double mastectomy at Stanford Hospital on March 2, 2009, followed by chemotherapy and radiation therapy. She was given "an excellent prognosis for a full recovery." Early in her campaign for the United States Senate seat held by Barbara Boxer, Fiorina humorously told a group of supporters: "I have to say that after chemotherapy, Barbara Boxer just isn't that scary anymore."

Fiorina married Todd Bartlem, a Stanford classmate, in June 1977. They divorced in 1984. In 1985, she married AT&T executive Frank Fiorina. It was the second marriage for each. They wanted to have children together but, as Fiorina put it, "That wasn't God's plan." She helped raise his two daughters, Traci and Lori Ann. Lori Ann struggled with alcoholism, substance abuse and bulimia. She died in 2009 at age 35.

Fiorina eyes are focused, her jaws set, as she looks directly into your eyes and tells you why your position should be the same as hers. She did this in a debate with Senator Barbara Boxer and apparently was not that convincing to the voters in California. Fiorina holds the position that the only thing that can beat "big government" is "big business." She is knowledgeable with a slight air of superiority. She is approachable and compassionate toward the plight of women in the workplace. Her capacity to assimilate concepts and articulate them in a clear and direct way to an audience makes her an important member of the conservative wing of the Republican Party.

The question, however, is how electable the conservative wing of the Republican Party is in 2016. Fiorina's ability to argue jobs, fairness in the workplace, and women's rights makes her an attractive candidate in the 2016 election.

CHAPTER 14

JIM GILMORE

"THE INQUISITOR"

An honest fighter who won't get a "title shot" due to his lackluster demeanor.

BACKGROUND INFORMATION

Current job	President CEO of the Free Congress Foundation
Born	October 6, 1949 in Richmond, VA
Religion	Methodist
Family	Roxane Gatling (m. 1977) Children: Jay, Ashton

PREVIOUS EXPERIENCE

James Stuart "Jim" Gilmore, III is the son of Margaret Evelyn Kandle, a church secretary, and James Stuart Gilmore, Jr., a grocery store meat cutter.

Gilmore graduated from John Randolph Tucker High School and received an undergraduate degree from the University of Virginia in 1971. He enlisted in the United States Army after attending college, receiving training and preparation for service in the Military Intelligence Corps at the newly created United States Army Intelligence Center at Fort Huachuca in Arizona. Gilmore also received rigorous foreign language education at the United States Defense Language Institute in Monterey, California.

Gilmore then worked for three years in the early 1970s in the 650th Military Intelligence Group. Serving in West Germany during the Vietnam War and fluent in German, he served as a U.S. Army Counterintelligence Agent. After his service in the U.S. Army, Gilmore entered the University of Virginia Law School in the mid-1970s, graduating in 1977.

After working for a decade as an attorney, Gilmore was elected Commonwealth's Attorney for his native Henrico County in 1987 and 1991, and then was first elected to statewide office in 1993 as Virginia's 38th Attorney General. Gilmore resigned in 1997 to run for governor, also joining the law firm of LeClairRyan as a partner. From 1998 until 2002, he was the 68th Governor of Virginia.

In 2007 Gilmore officially announced that he would run in the race for the 2008 presidency. Due to difficulty of raising enough money, he ended his campaign.

He went on to run for the U.S. Senate in 2008. He was defeated, only carrying four counties in the state. In many cases, he lost in many areas of the state that were reliably Republican.

Gilmore has also served as Chairman of the National Council on

Readiness & Preparedness, a homeland security program focused on community involvement and public/private partnerships. Additionally, Gilmore is on the Board of Directors of the National Rifle Association and is a political commentator on Fox News.

GOODFIELD PERSONALITY TYPING
TYPE 3.2 THE INQUISITOR
I am on my way so get out of my way - please

First Impression

- Outspoken
- Powerful and opinionated
- Cocky and self-assured
- Approachable and bombastic
- Can be really tough
- Outwardly open, inwardly closed
- Believes in his direction
- A fighter

Photo Courtesy of Gage Skidmore

Five reasons why this person is the Inquisitor type 3.2

1. One eyebrow up
2. Shifting of jaws (smoking behavior)
3. Eyes closing, but not completely (distrust)
4. Difference between left and right side of mouth
5. Blocked breathing

Symbolic Level of Non-Verbal Leak

SL 1 - Pain/fear

SL 2 - Anger

SL 3 - Control by
- cynicism
- swallowing down
- calculated emotional response

PHOTO COURTESY OF GAGE SKIDMORE

Non-Verbal Leak (NVL)
- Eyes open
- Eyes shiny
- Shifting of jaws
- Eyebrow(s) up
- Building up pressure around mouth
- Mouth open
- Showing teeth
- Mouth closed
- Eyes closing, but not completely (distrust)
- Swallow down
- Eyes open

Unconscious Meaning of the NVL
"I am in pain and fear, and that makes me angry. I don't feel authorized to express it. I swallow it down and smile. My question is shall I show this … or distance myself?"

PSYCHOLOGICAL OBSERVATION AND PUBLIC COMMENTS

Governor Gilmore is outspoken, tough, powerful, bombastic, opinionated, cocky and self-assured. He is approachable, outwardly open and inwardly closed.

Gilmore believes in his direction; and as governor, he did his best to keep his campaign promises — and he did!

Gilmore is an individual who is ready for a fight when his basic views and values are challenged. He is a "scrapper," unafraid to express his aggression, particularly around the issue of injustice. He has a lot of blocked aggression, which shows most clearly as very well-developed masseter muscles in his jaw.

Gilmore takes his aggressive impulses and directs them at the injustice he perceives. He is two-valued in his orientation, seeing many issues as either black or white. He chooses his fights carefully. The biggest issue in his life is that of justice versus injustice.

Governor Gilmore is politically well-connected, but his lack of name recognition, and general lack of openness to difference and his rigidity, make him an unlikely candidate on a national level. One thing is for sure, if you're in a fight and need a warrior who will not quit and back you all the way, Governor Jim Gilmore would be a very good choice!

Governor Gilmore sees himself as a realistic candidate for the Republican nomination. Even though he is strong and able to articulate his views, he faces an uphill battle. However, he has the courage and willingness to continue as long as his candidacy is viable.

Gilmore has a vision for a different America, one that will return America to the policies of a dynamic, entrepreneurial free-market economy and a policy of peace-through-strength for our national security.

CHAPTER 15

LINDSEY GRAHAM

PHOTO COURTESY OF GAGE SKIDMORE

"THE DOUBTER"

A pro-military senator interested in bipartisan straight talk.

BACKGROUND INFORMATION

Current job	U.S. Senator from South Carolina
Born	July 9, 1955 in Central, SC
Religion	Southern Baptist
Family	Never married

PREVIOUS EXPERIENCE

Senator Lindsey Graham is the son of Millie and Florence James "F.J." Graham. His father ran a restaurant-bar-pool hall-liquor store, the Sanitary Cafe. Graham became the first member of his family to attend college, and he joined the Reserve Officers' Training Corps. When he was 21 years old, his mother died of Hodgkin's lymphoma at age 52, and his father died 15 months later of a heart attack at age 69. Because his then 13-year-old sister was left orphaned, the military allowed Graham to attend University of South Carolina in Columbia so he could be near home and care for his sister, whom he adopted. Graham never married. If elected president, Graham would be the first bachelor president elected since James Buchanan in 1856.

Graham graduated from the University of South Carolina with a B.A. in Psychology in 1977, and from the University of South Carolina School of Law with a J.D. in 1981. Graham joined the U.S. Air Force in 1984. He was sent to Europe as a military prosecutor and defense attorney in Frankfurt, Germany. After four years in Europe, he returned to South Carolina and then left active duty in 1989. He subsequently entered private practice as a lawyer.

Graham joined the South Carolina Air National Guard in 1989, where he served until 1995, and then joined the U.S. Air Force Reserve. Between January 1995 and January 2005, Graham's military work totaled 108 hours, an average of less than a day and a half per year. He was an Air Force Reserve appellate judge during part of the period.

In 2007, Graham served in Iraq as a reservist on active duty for a short period in April and for two weeks in August, working on detainee and rule-of-law issues. He also served in Afghanistan during the August 2009 Senate recess. In 2015, Graham retired as a Colonel from the Air Force with more than 33 years of service, after reaching the statutory retirement age of 60 for his rank.

GOODFIELD PERSONALITY TYPING
TYPE 3 THE DOUBTER
Searching for the truth with a big "T"

First Impression
- Experienced
- Open-minded
- Reasonable
- Approachable
- Well-informed
- Friendly
- Knows Washington politics

U.S. Senate Portrait

Five reasons why this person is the Doubter type 3
1. Eyebrows up
2. Teariness and tightening eyelids (squinting)
3. Somewhat developed jaws
4. Tongue out/in
5. Blocked breathing

Symbolic Level of Non-Verbal Leak

SL 1 - Disbelief/pain
SL 2 - Anger
SL 3 - Control by:
- intellectualization
- calculated emotional response

Official U.S. Senate photo

Non-Verbal Leak (NVL)
- Eyes open
- Eyebrows up
- Eyes closed
- Teariness and tightening eyelids (squinting)
- Somewhat developed jaws

- Tension upper lip
- Pressing lips
- Blocked breathing
- Tongue out/in
- Eyes open

Unconscious Meaning of the NVL

"I am in pain, and I don't belief what happened to me. I am angry. I'm not authorized to express it, so I control it by holding in and intellectualization."

PSYCHOLOGICAL OBSERVATION AND PUBLIC COMMENTS

Senator Lindsey Graham is a bright, articulate, conservative spokesman for the Republican Party. His strong but rigid views on American foreign policy are well-known. He is frustrated by others with different viewpoints or differing experiences regarding international affairs. With more than 30 trips to the Middle East, he is extremely well-informed about what he sees as the correct solutions to the Middle East conflicts.

Graham is a "peace through strength" advocate. This leads to some difficulty in relationships, as he has no self-doubt about the right direction. To some he is a charismatic leader who has a corner on "the truth." Graham is a strong driving force in selling his positions. He believes his positions are well-thought-out especially considering his worldly experiences. If you're looking for passion in this man, you must look to his politics, that's where you will find it. It's more in the office than at home.

Senator Graham's bipartisan approach and years of experience can hopefully set the tone for a less polarized electoral debate. That is assuming he will qualify to be in the debate process, as he has garnered little support as a presidential candidate. He is a bridge-builder with strength and a desire to communicate on a bipartisan basis. His statements about greenhouse gases, and their impact on the environment, have not made him the most popular person with his Republican colleagues.

Graham is a systematic, strong-willed, hard-working individual with high expectations of himself and others. He has the capacity for great leadership. As a person, he is a perfectionist. When he looks at an issue, he realizes the short-term goal and the long-term objectives. He can't give up what is now for what might be later. He is approachable and a reasonable negotiator.

Senator Graham shows his aggression on a nonverbal level by putting his tongue out quickly, withdrawing it and closing his eyes. He has managed to skillfully communicate his differences regarding important issues facing America. In the finest sense of the words, he is a "Southern politician."

Graham is smooth, pleasant; however, he does not forget his objectives. His candidacy will bring two things into the race: an ability to promote bipartisan communication regarding important issues facing our country, and his concern about strengthening America's military. These two items should be a part of the debate in 2016. The question: is he the best spokesman for these concerns?

CHAPTER 16

MIKE HUCKABEE

PHOTO COURTESY OF GAGE SKIDMORE

"THE DOER"

A talented "down-homeboy" with the big, uptown ideas.

BACKGROUND INFORMATION

Current job	Author, commentator, public speaker
Born	August 24, 1955 in Hope, AR
Religion	Southern Baptist
Family	Janet McCain (m. 1974) John Mark, David, Sarah

PREVIOUS EXPERIENCE

Governor Mike Huckabee is the son of Dorsey Wiles Huckabee and his wife Mae Elder Huckabee, both conservative Southern Democrats. Huckabee is of English ancestry, with roots in America dating to the colonial era. He has cited his working-class upbringing as the reason for his political views; his father worked as a fireman and mechanic, and his mother worked as a clerk at a gas company.

His first job, when he was 14, was at a radio station where he read the news and weather. He graduated magna cum laude from Ouachita Baptist University, completing his bachelor's degree in Religion in two-and-a-half years. He then attended Southwestern Baptist Theological Seminary in Fort Worth, Texas. He dropped out of the seminary after one year in order to take a job in Christian broadcasting.

At age 21, Huckabee was a staffer for televangelist James Robison. Prior to his political career, Huckabee served as pastor at Immanuel Baptist Church in Pine Bluff, Arkansas from 1980 to 1986, and the Beech Street Baptist Church in Texarkana from 1986 to 1992.

Within two years of their marriage, Huckabee's wife Janet was diagnosed with spinal cancer. She underwent surgery and six weeks of radiation therapy. She eventually recovered.

Huckabee started 24-hour television stations in both Pine Bluff and Texarkana, where he produced documentaries and hosted a program called Positive Alternatives. He encouraged the all-white Immanuel Baptist Church to accept black members in the mid-1980s. Huckabee served as president of the Arkansas Baptist State Convention from 1989 to 1991.

Huckabee served twice as Arkansas lieutenant governor. From 1996 - 2007 he was the 44th governor of Arkansas.

This is the second time Huckabee is running in a presidential election campaign. The first time was in 2008. He withdrew from seeking the candidacy as it became apparent he would lose in Texas. Huckabee finished the race with an estimated 248 pledged delegates.

Huckabee plays the electric bass guitar in his classic-rock cover band, Capitol Offense. Until recently, he hosted the *Huckabee* talkshow on the Fox News.

GOODFIELD PERSONALITY TYPING
TYPE 2 THE DOER
Boundary Checker

First Impression
- Fun and funny
- Experienced TV personality
- Desperate for contact on some level
- Intelligent and reluctant
- Talented and informed
- Personable and wants to please
- Hiding something

Photo Courtesy of Gage Skidmore

Five reasons why this person is a Doer type 2
1. Eyes wide open
2. Very pronounced jaws
3. Tongue out
4. Pressured defiant appearance
5. Tension in shoulders

Non-Verbal Leak (NVL)

- Eyes open
- Eyes wide open
- Pronounced jaws sometimes pulsing
- Tongue in/out quick
- Tightening of the mouth
- High breathing
- Lines throat deeper
- Concentration lines stronger
- Movement of the shoulders
- Eyes close not completely (one eye more than the other)
- Eyes open

Unconscious Meaning of the NVL

"I feel denied, and that makes me angry. I try not to express it, so I swallow those feelings down, until they come out later — and they really do!

PSYCHOLOGICAL OBSERVATION AND PUBLIC COMMENTS

Governor Huckabee is a magnificent manipulator. He is full of drive, direction and purpose, an inspirational dynamo. Underneath this celebrity is a man who can be explosive, if he's really honest with his feelings. Although he can be suddenly explosive, he is quick to reevaluate and adapt to the needs and demands of his constituency with his remarks about the world that he sees and is selling.

Governor Huckabee is intuitive about the needs of others. After all, it is in his DNA. He is an ordained Southern Baptist minister. It's always been the Bible and broadcasting, one way or another.

As much as Huckabee is bombastic, outgoing, and involved, his deeper feelings are reserved for a very select audience. His verbal skills are persuasive. His energy and genuine enthusiasm make him a dynamo where his goals are concerned. He is intuitive and compassionate. For Huckabee, action is more of a priority than intimacy.

Beneath that polished exterior is a man who has seen much pain. Huckabee is a man of the people who can, and does, identify with people who are living in hard times and are trying to survive. The values that he gained from his parents come through in his discussions and presentations about the way he sees the world, and the solutions necessary to address the wrongs about which he speaks.

Whether it be with a guitar in his hand, or microphone in front of him spouting his brand of philosophy, compassion and deep understanding of human needs, Governor Huckabee is a viable candidate for a nation divided and in economic trouble. It would be a major decision on the part of the Republican Party to make that diagnosis of America and her needs. An even greater decision on the part of the American public is to vote for a man with heart, strong will and an old-fashioned vision.

Governor Huckabee is a media savvy, witty and articulate spokesman for his conservative viewpoint. His years of radio and television show finiteness his debating and public engagement skills. The primary question is, however, with all of this ability to communicate his message in an accurate and clear way, is anybody really interested in endorsing it with their vote?

In 2016, is there a space on the national an international level for a "Good 'Ol Boy" when issues such as nuclear proliferation, treaties, and moves by Vladimir Putin are being discussed and decided? It is one thing to laugh and to appreciate wit, it is quite another to sit across a symbolic table with hardliners bent on imposing their will.

CHAPTER 17

BOBBY JINDAL

PHOTO COURTESY OF GAGE SKIDMORE

"THE DOER"

Eastern roots, Southern charm, a smart man with a plan.

BACKGROUND INFORMATION

Current job	Governor of Louisiana
Born	June 10, 1971 in Baton Rouge, LA
Religion	Catholic
Family	Supriya Jolly (m. 1997) Children: Selia Elizabeth, Shaan Robert, Slade Ryan

PREVIOUS EXPERIENCE

Piyush "Bobby" Jindal is the son of Amar and Raj Jindal, immigrants from Punjab, India. His father, Amar Jindal, is a civil engineer and Raj Gupta worked in nuclear physics in Chandigarh. Prior to immigrating to the United States, both his parents were lecturers at an Indian engineering college. Jindal's paternal grandfather was a Khanpur merchant, and his maternal grandfather was a Ferozepur banker.

Jindal graduated in 1988 from high school at the top of his class. He graduated from Brown University in 1991 at the age of 20, with honors in two majors, biology and public policy. Jindal applied to and was accepted by both Harvard Medical School and Yale Law School, but he chose a study at New College, Oxford, as a Rhodes Scholar. He received an M.Litt. degree in political science with an emphasis in health policy from the University of Oxford in 1994.

Jindal's interest in Christianity was formed in high school. He began attending church, and in the fall of 1989 he was baptized a Roman Catholic.

Governor Murphy Foster appointed Jindal in 1996 as Secretary of the Louisiana Department of Health and Hospitals, an agency that represented about 40 percent of the state budget and employed more than12,000 people. Jindal was 24 at the time. During his tenure, Louisiana's Medicaid program went from bankruptcy with a $400 million deficit into three years of surpluses totaling $220 million. In 1998, Jindal was appointed executive director of the National Bipartisan Commission on the Future of Medicare, a 17-member panel charged with devising plans to reform Medicare.

At 28 years of age in 1999, Jindal was appointed to become the youngest-ever president of the University of Louisiana System, the nation's 16th largest system of higher education with more than 80,000 students per year.

In 2001, Jindal was nominated by President George W. Bush to be Assistant Secretary of Health and Human Services for Planning and Evaluation. He resigned from that post on February 21, 2003, to return to Louisiana and run for governor. Jindal came to national prominence during the 2003 election for Louisiana governor. Despite his losing the election in 2003, the run for governor made Jindal a well-known figure on the state's political scene and a rising star within the Republican Party.

From 2005-2008, Jindal was a member of the U.S. House of Representatives. In 2008 he became the 55th Governor of Louisiana.

GOODFIELD PERSONALITY TYPING
TYPE 2 THE DOER
Boundary Checker

First Impression

- A dreamer with a plan
- A pleasant pusher
- Pressured speech
- Witty and quick
- Well-informed true believer
- A man who has something to prove

Photo Courtesy of Gage Skidmore

Five reasons why this person is a Doer type 2

1. Eyes wide open
1. Very pronounced jaws
2. Tongue out
3. Pressured defiant appearance
4. Tension in shoulders

Non-Verbal Leak (NVL)
- Eyes open
- Eyes wide open
- Pronounced jaws sometimes pulsing
- Tongue in/out quick
- Tightening of the mouth
- High breathing
- Lines throat deeper
- Concentration lines stronger Movement of the shoulders
- Eyes close not completely (one eye more not completely closed)
- Eyes open

Unconscious Meaning of the NVL
"I feel unnoticed, and that makes me angry. I try not to express it, so I swallow those feelings down, until they come out later. And they really do!"

PSYCHOLOGICAL OBSERVATION AND PUBLIC COMMENTS

Governor Bobby Jindal is a man of purpose, drive and direction. He is skilled in presenting his view of reality. He is skilled in influencing others to see his view and the reasons why they should adopt his policies. Most of the time he is able to control his anger. Sometimes are easier than others. He is, however, quick to evaluate and adapt.

Jindal is a clear thinker and well-informed with regard to the needs of his constituents. On some level he has some difficulty with contact. He is however, a great salesman of his ideas and viewpoints. He has a subtle charm and some reluctance to present his deeper feelings which are masked from himself and others rather well. He is not very spontaneous and enjoys the pleasure of his own company.

Governor Jindal is a charismatic "True Believer." That's the good news and the bad news at the same time. He is totally committed to his conservative position, which apparently resonates to enough constituents to have him elected to Congress, as well as the Governor's mansion in Louisiana.

Jindal is extremely bright and articulate. However, his "pressured speech" can give others the impression he is a person who is thinking faster then he can speak. The impact of this on the audience gives the feeling of being "rained on" by the wisdom he possesses. He is absolutely a man with a plan, one that has had some degree of success in his native Louisiana. His ability to translate that plan into a national platform, understood and accepted by America, is his big challenge.

The primary problem he faces is his seemingly two valued orientation - namely, his ability to dismiss others as ignorant, foolhardy or simply not seeing America for what it is or can be.

The question is, can he speak to and resonate with a larger group of Americans with diverse backgrounds and different philosophies on what is right for America?

Louisiana is not New York or California. His views, although expressed in an articulate, well-thought-out way, are unlikely to generate enough enthusiasm to put his name forward over those of fellow Republicans with more name recognition.

CHAPTER 18

JOHN KASICH

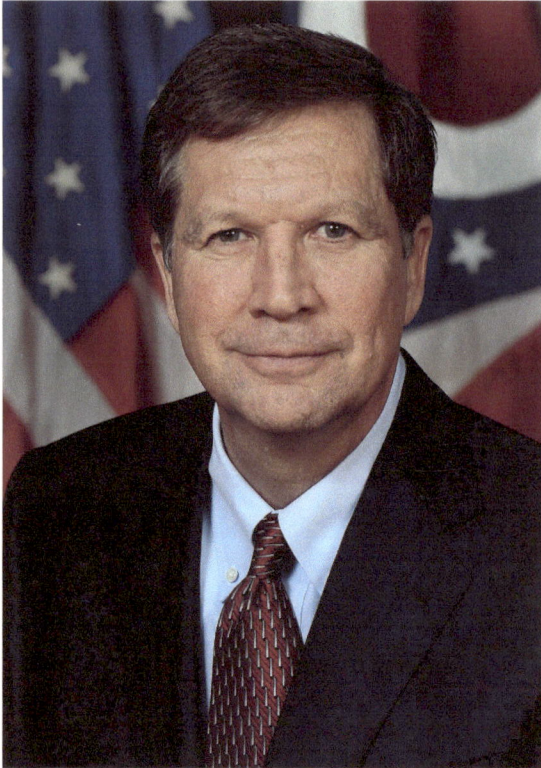

PHOTO COURTESY OF GAGE SKIDMORE

"THE DOUBTER"

He's not charismatic, but, an informed nice guy who knows D.C. politics.

BACKGROUND INFORMATION

Current job	Governor of Ohio
Born	May 13, 1952 in McKees Rocks, PA
Religion	Anglican
Family	Mary Lee Griffith (m. 1975–80)
	Karen Waldbillig (m. 1997)
	Children: Emma, Reese

PREVIOUS EXPERIENCE

Governor John Kasich is the son of Anne Vukovich and John Kasich, who worked as a mail carrier. Kasich's father was of Czech descent, while his mother was of Croatian ancestry. Both his father and mother were children of immigrants. Kasich described himself as "a Croatian and a Czech."

As a freshman at Ohio State University, he wrote a letter of admiration to President Richard Nixon, requesting a meeting with the President. The letter was delivered to Nixon by the University's president Novice Fawcett and Kasich was granted a 20-minute meeting with Nixon in December 1970.

After earning a Bachelor of Arts degree in political science from Ohio State in 1974, he went on to work as a researcher for the Ohio Legislative Service Commission. From 1975 to 1978, he served as an administrative assistant to then-state Senator Buz Lukens.

At age 26, Kasich was elected to the Ohio Senate. From 1983-2001, he was a member of the U.S. House of Representatives. For six years he was the Chairman of the House Budget Committee. In 2011 Kasich became the 69th Governor of Ohio.

Kasich has a strong background in the executive branch of government as a twice- elected governor. He has a vast background in international foreign affairs from his many years in the United States Congress serving on important House committees, such as the Armed Services Committee. In 1995, when Kasich assumed the position of Budget Chairman, the U.S. Federal Budget had a deficit of roughly $163 billion, and upon the conclusion of his tenure as Budget Chairman, the U.S. Federal Budget had a surplus of more than $236 billion.

Kasich was a commentator on Fox News, hosting *Heartland with John*

Kasich from 2001 to 2007. And guest-hosting *The O'Reilly Factor*, filling in for Bill O'Reilly as needed. Kasich also frequently appeared as a guest host and analyst on *Hannity & Colmes* (the title of which was later changed to *Hannity*). He also worked as an investment banker, as managing director of Lehman Brothers' Columbus, Ohio office.

Although he considers denominations irrelevant, Kasich was raised a Catholic and has stated that "there's always going to be a part of me that considers myself a Catholic." He drifted away from his religion as an adult, but he came to embrace an Anglican faith after both his parents were killed in a car crash by a drunk driver.

GOODFIELD PERSONALITY TYPING
TYPE 3 THE DOUBTER
Searching for the truth with a big "T"

First Impression

- Compassionate
- Open-minded
- Reasonable
- Approachable
- Well-informed
- Friendly
- Knows Washington politics

Photo Courtesy of Gage Skidmore

Five reasons why this person is the Doubter type 3

1. Eyebrows up
2. Teariness and tightening eyelids (squinting)
3. Somewhat developed jaws
4. Tongue out/in
5. Blocked breathing

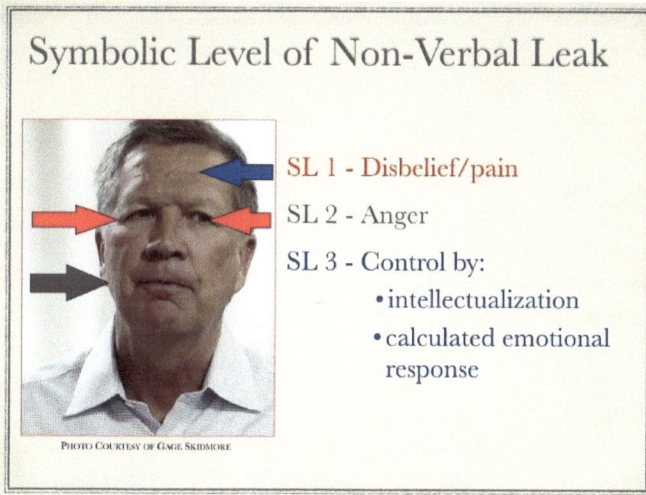

Symbolic Level of Non-Verbal Leak

SL 1 - Disbelief/pain
SL 2 - Anger
SL 3 - Control by:
  • intellectualization
  • calculated emotional response

PHOTO COURTESY OF GAGE SKIDMORE

Non-Verbal Leak (NVL)
- Eyes open
- Eyebrows up
- Eyes closed
- Eyes open
- Teariness and tightening eyelids (squinting)
- Somewhat developed jaws Tension upper lip
- Pressing lips
- Blocked breathing
- Tongue out/in
- Eyes open

Unconscious Meaning of the NVL
"*I am in pain, and I don't belief what has happened. I am angry. I'm not authorized to express it, so I control it by holding in and intellectualization.*"

PSYCHOLOGICAL OBSERVATION AND PUBLIC COMMENTS

Governor John Kasich is "Mr. Common Sense." He is an experienced, approachable, well-informed nice guy who really knows Washington politics. He is not charismatic, but the way he speaks and explains his views is interesting and refreshing. Is that charismatic?

Kasich is clearly bright with a gentle power that can be overlooked by those giving him a cursory glance. His logic, reason and high expectation of himself and others have accomplished a lot in his state and in Washington. He is a quiet man who gets frustrated at others' lack of performance. Moreover, he radiates an easy Midwest approach to difference. He is approachable and yet opinionated, with a willingness to understand and compromise.

Governor Kasich is a hard worker who seeks fairness and balance in the projects in which he is involved. He has demonstrated the capacity to work both sides of the aisle. He is on some levels approachable; however, he is reluctant to share his deeper feelings and frustrations with others.

Although unassuming and quiet, Kasich is a keen observer and a good judge of character. The faults and frailty of others do not slip by him. This is the difficulty in some of his relationships as others failed to live up to his high standards.

Kasich is generally approachable and friendly, but true intimacy with him is often transitory and elusive. On a deeper level there is some self-doubt and a concern of rejection. This has not stopped him from reaching important leadership positions.

The successes that Kasich has achieved are on some level motivated by his concern about failure and living up to the exceptionally high expectations he has for himself. He has demonstrated a gentle but effective style of leadership.

Kasich is admired by others for his consistency, directness and simple honesty. Those in the political arena who are more manipulative and divisive find Kasich somewhat of an enigma. He seeks fairness over opportunity and good judgment over expediency. In that sense, to some with differing agendas and approaches, he is frequently misunderstood.

Governor Kasich is a well experienced individual in both government and business. He is a "people person," with compassion and concern in his long history of service to state and country.

Kasich has a strong religious philosophy which is a guide to his political and moral stances. He prides himself in his ability to communicate with both sides of the aisle. Although a Republican he is able to understand and occasionally support positions held by other groups. His reaction to difference makes him an attractive person in this crowded race for the White House.

CHAPTER 19

PETER KING

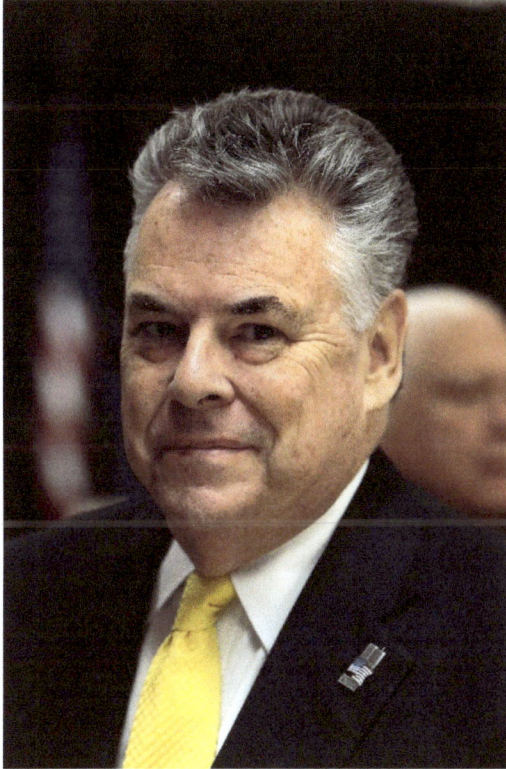

PHOTO COURTESY OF GAGE SKIDMORE

"THE INQUISITOR"

A NYC street-fighter. A pained person promising programs for D.C.

BACKGROUND INFORMATION

Current job	Congressman U.S. House of Representative
Born	April 5, 1944 in New York, NY
Religion	Catholic
Family	Rosemary Wiedl (m. 1967) Children: 2

PREVIOUS EXPERIENCE

Peter Thomas "Pete" King was born in Manhattan and raised in Sunnyside, Queens, New York. He was the son of Ethel M. Gittins King and Peter E. King, who was a New York City police officer. His grandparents came from Irish and Welsh heritage. He graduated from St. Francis College in 1965 with a degree in political science, and he earned his J.D. from Notre Dame Law School in Indiana in 1968. That same year, he began service in the 165th Infantry Regiment of the New York Army National Guard. He worked for the Nassau County District Attorney's Office until 1974, when he was honorably discharged from the 165th Infantry Regiment.

Before serving in county government, Representative King had extensive experience as a practicing attorney and civic leader. He began his political career in November 1977.

Congressman King is serving his 12th term in the U.S. House of Representative.

King is a member of the Homeland Security Committee and Chairman of the Sub-Committee on Counterterrorism and Intelligence. He also serves on the Financial Services Committee and Permanent Select Committee on Intelligence. Congressman King, who previously served as Chairman of the Committee in 2005-2006 and again in 2011-2012, has been a leader in the ongoing effort to have Homeland Security funding based on threat analysis. He is a strong supporter of the war against international terrorism, both at home and abroad. As Chairman of the Homeland Security Committee, he stood up to the pressure from special interest groups and the media to hold a series of hearings on Islamic radicalization.

During his years in Congress, King has attained a reputation for being well-informed and independent. Congressman King is a strong supporter of law enforcement and our military, and he has fought hard to bring veterans' benefits into the 21st century. Congressman King is also a strong supporter of funding to combat deadly illnesses such as breast cancer and prostate cancer.

GOODFIELD PERSONALITY TYPING
TYPE 3.2 THE INQUISITOR
I am on my way so get out of my way - please

First Impression

- Outspoken and tough
- Powerful and opinionated
- Cocky and self-assured
- Approachable and bombastic
- Outwardly open, inwardly closed
- Believes in his direction
- A fighter

Photo Courtesy of
Gage Skidmore

Five reasons why this person is the Inquisitor type 3.2

1. One eyebrow up
2. Shifting of jaws (smoking behavior)
3. Eyes closing, but not completely (distrust)
4. Difference between left and right side of mouth
5. Blocked breathing

Symbolic Level of Non-Verbal Leak

SL 1 - Pain/fear

SL 2 - Anger

SL 3 - Control by:
- smiling it away
- intellectualization

PHOTO COURTESY OF GAGE SKIDMORE

Non-Verbal Leak (NVL)
- Eyes open
- Eyes shiny
- Shifting of jaws
- Eyebrow(s) up
- Building up pressure around mouth
- Mouth open
- Showing teeth
- Mouth closed
- Eyes closing, but not completely (distrust)
- Swallow down
- Eyes open

Unconscious Meaning of the NVL
"I am in pain and fear, and that makes me angry. I don't feel authorized to express it so I smile and swallow it down."

PSYCHOLOGICAL OBSERVATION AND PUBLIC COMMENTS

Congressman Peter King is outspoken, tough, powerful, opinionated, cocky, bombastic, pragmatic and self-assured. And… he is a New Yorker! If there is a stereotypical New York politician, it is this man. He says what he thinks and is not afraid of a fight. Controversy is his middle name. King is "street smart" and "fox quick." He wears his heart on his sleeve. He hides his political science and law degrees behind a cunning smile and a razor wit.

King doesn't like people who hurt or threaten other people. He is outwardly open but inwardly closed. He carries a lot of the pain of others who have been wronged. He's a good guy to have on your side in a fight!

Congressman King is a man who prides himself in knowing the people from his congressional district and in up holding their needs and rights in Congress. He is a "good ol' boy" with a good old heart. He is a man of principle who takes injustice not just to himself but to his constituents personally.

King's working class background has bonded him closely with the people he represents. King is patriotic and a determined winner, hostile and combative toward any and all who would fight against his constituents or the America he loves so much. He can be explosive when pushed too far. He loves to fight for the underdog. He never forgets his roots! In that sense, he is an anomaly. He is an old-fashioned guy, fighting for old-fashioned principles in an age of iPhones and ISIS.

If America is looking for another Jimmy Stewart from the movie "Mr. Smith goes to Washington," they could find him in an angry man with tears in his eyes looking for reason and justice. His name is Peter King. He probably realizes that his run for the White House is a futile act, but that never stopped him before.

CHAPTER 20

MARTIN O'MALLEY

PHOTO COURTESY CREATIVE COMMONS

"THE PREVAILER"

A JFK impersonator longing to re-create "Camelot" in 2016.

BACKGROUND INFORMATION

Current job	Visiting Professor Johns Hopkins University's Carey Business School
Born	January 18, 1963 in Washington, D.C.
Religion	Catholic
Family	Katie Curran (m. 1990) Children: Grace, Tara, William, Jack

PREVIOUS EXPERIENCE

Martin Joseph O'Malley is the son of Barbara Suelzer and Thomas Martin O'Malley. His father served as a bombardier in the U.S. Army Air Force during the Second World War (it was said he witnessed the mushroom cloud rise over Hiroshima while on a routine mission). O'Malley's father was of Irish descent and his mother from Irish, German, Dutch, and Scottish ancestry. He later became a Montgomery County-based criminal defense lawyer, and an assistant United States Attorney for the District of Columbia.

Governor O'Malley attended The Catholic University of America, graduating in 1985. Later that year he enrolled at the University of Maryland School of Law, earning his J.D. in 1988 and passing the bar that same year. O'Malley was hired as an assistant state's attorney for the City of Baltimore, holding that position until 1990.

From 1991 to 1999, he was elected to the Baltimore City Council to represent the 3rd district. As councilman, he served as Chairman of the Legislative Investigations Committee and Chairman of the Taxation and Finance Committee.

O'Malley became the 47th mayor of Baltimore in 1999, and served until 2007.

From 2007 to 2015, O'Malley served as the 61st governor of Maryland. During his term, he signed a bill that repealed the death penalty in Maryland for all future offenders. He also signed a new gun control bill into law. He endorsed tougher enforcement against illegal immigration by the federal government. O'Malley signed a law that would make the children of illegal immigrants eligible for in-state college tuition under certain conditions.

O'Malley has been called the Rock 'n' Roll Governor for his membership in the Celtic Rock Band "O'Malley's March" since 1988. He plays the banjo, guitar and sings.

GOODFIELD PERSONALITY TYPING
TYPE 2.0 THE PREVAILER
Welcome to the wonderful world of me and mine

First Impression
- Charismatic man
- Complete gentleman
- Open to difference
- Compassionate
- Clever and witty
- A John F. Kennedy type

Photo by Tom
Williams/Roll Call

Five reasons why this person is a Prevailer type 2.0
1. Eyes (anger/trance)
2. One elevated eyebrow
3. Eyes that close but not completely
4. Head on angle (provocative)
5. Left/right shoulder difference

Symbolic Level of Non-Verbal Leak

SL 1 - Shock
SL 2 - Anger
SL 3 - Control by:
- biting on lip
- swallowing down
- calculated seductive response

Photo Wikimedia

Non-Verbal Leak (NVL)
- Eyes open
- Eyes shiny and wide open
- Shifting of jaws
- Pressure built up around the mouth
- Mouth open

- Teeth showing
- Mouth closed
- Eyes closing, but not completely (distrust)
- Swallow down
- Eyes open

Unconscious Meaning of the NVL
"I am alone and in pain, and that makes me angry. I distrust those feelings so I swallow them down, put on a fake smile and seduce those around me."

PSYCHOLOGICAL OBSERVATION AND PUBLIC COMMENTS

In the right time and right place, Governor O'Malley would be a natural candidate for the White House. He is the most JFK-like of person to seek the presidency since the original JFK. Bright, charismatic and articulate with that shy, seductive, disarming humor, he would be quite the member of a 2016 Democratic ticket.

Perhaps he will be a vice presidential candidate with all of the exposure, making him more viable in 2020. He might just be what the Democrats are looking for, and they just might fit perfectly into his plans.

O'Malley is a man with a plan, and it definitely includes higher public office. Perhaps not now, but one would be foolish to count him out of a return trip to his birthplace of Washington D.C. Just like John Kennedy, he was born for the media age and is skilled at its use!

Governor O'Malley is an Irish Catholic musician with his own Celtic band. O'Malley could just sing and play his way into the White House just like an Irish Pied Piper ridding Washington of partisan rats and bringing hope back to Camelot. That looks a little optimistic for 2016.

Governor O'Malley is focused on his needs, goals, and objectives. Perhaps the strongest feeling about him is his charm, compassion and approachability. He is comfortable in front of an audience. He is intuitive and persistent when it comes to serving the needs of others. O'Malley is a natural salesman for the downtrodden for whom he advocates with his style, charm and smile.

O'Malley is a charming, smooth-talker and in that sense a natural communicator. As a person and as a politician he is persuasive and goal-oriented. He is skilled at the art of articulation and influence. He is more oriented toward action than intimacy. On a deep level there's a fundamental distrust of others. If you know him well you may be aware of this about him.

O'Malley suffers the same problem as many of the contenders —

national name- recognition and party appreciation. Bernie Sanders has successfully sucked the air out of O'Malley's balloon as the logical alternative to Hillary Clinton.

There are three things necessary to start a fire: oxygen, fuel and heat. This combustion triangle explains the dilemma that good, qualified men and women face as they attempt to get national attention to their views values and desires for America. The oxygen is the exposure to the media. The fuel is the power position of a strong individual. The heat is the degree of excitement and interest that the individual creates on a national level and also on a personal level.

This simple combination so simple may very well be driving away people that our founding fathers envisioned as those who would lead our country on further steps towards democracy. Governor O'Malley may possess greatness, as other candidates may as well, but the fire may never burn.

O'Malley will be nothing more than an afterthought in a predictable election. At least this is true for the perception on the part of the Democratic Party. At least for now, Camelot will have to wait.

O'Malley is the only Prevailer type 2.0 running for President in 2016.

CHAPTER 21

GEORGE PATAKI

PHOTO WIKIPEDIA CREATIVE COMMONS

"THE PLOTTER"

A tired war-horse never willing to quit, always trying to be relevant.

BACKGROUND INFORMATION

Current job	Lawyer and politician
Born	June 24, 1945
Birthplace	Peekskill, New York
Religion	Roman Catholicism
Family	Libby Rowland (m. 1973) Children Emily, Teddy, Allison and George Owen

PREVIOUS EXPERIENCE

George Pataki is the son of Louis P. Pataki (1912–1996), a mailman volunteer fire chief who also ran the Pataki Farm, and Margaret Lagana Pataki. Pataki grew up in upstate New York working on the family farm where he learned the power of discipline, community, and hard work. His grandparents were immigrants from Hungarian, Irish and Italian ancestry.

After graduating from high school, Pataki entered Yale University with George W. Bush in 1964 on an academic scholarship and graduated in three years. While there he served as chairman of the Conservative Party of the Yale Political Union. He participated in debates. He received his J.D. from Columbia Law School in 1970.

While practicing law at Plunkett and Jaffe, P.C., he ran for Mayor of Peekskill in 1981 and won. From 1985 - 1992, he became a member of the New York Assembly. For one year he was a member of the New York Senate. Partaki became a three-term Governor from 1995 till 2006.

Governor Pataki has been a long-time advocate of tax cuts during his administration and his time in the state legislature. He signed and sponsored several tax cuts during his first term in office and additionally made spending cuts to the budgets he proposed. This has included a push for privatization of state entities.

After leaving the Governorship, Pataki joined the law firm Chadbourne & Parke in New York. In September 2007, he was appointed as a United States delegate to the United Nations. Pataki has formed an environmental consulting firm, the Pataki-Cahill Group, with his former chief of staff John Cahill, and works with the Council on Foreign Relations on climate change issues. He also serves as the vice-chairman of the board of directors for the American Security Council Foundation.

GOODFIELD PERSONALITY TYPING
TYPE 1.2 THE PLOTTER
Ambivalent about being present

Photo Courtesy of Gage
Skidmore

First Impression
- Lot of pain and sadness
- A tired man who won't quit
- Tired old soldier
- Old fashioned politician
- A man trying to be relevant

Five reasons why this person is a Plotter Type 1.2
1. Trance but not showing all the time
2. Eyes do not close completely
3. Eyebrows up
4. Tightness around the mouth
5. Mouth that is not completely closed

Symbolic Level of Non-Verbal Leak

SL 1 - Denial

SL 2 - Sadness
   Anger
   seen by cynicism

SL 3 - Control by:
   • holding back
   • trance

PHOTO COURTESY OF GAGE SKIDMORE

Non-Verbal Leak (NVL)
- Eyes open
- Teary partially open eyes
- Eyes closed
- Biting down
- Lines bilateral nose and mouth intensified
- Tension round the mouth

- Swallow down
- Eyes open

Unconscious Meaning of the NVL
"I am denying myself, that makes me sad and also angry. I do not trust myself expressing my feelings and that makes me unsure."

PSYCHOLOGICAL OBSERVATION AND PUBLIC COMMENTS

The nonverbal behavior of Governor Pataki shows a man in a trance much of the time. Occasionally fear and self-doubt show in his eyes. He compensates by trying to make bold remarks that come across flat without affect. The difference between the left and the right side of his mouth in others might suggest sarcasm or wit, but in his case it simply makes him look unsure. He says the right words, but there's no passion behind it. He comes across like an old warhorse who's fought many fights and won't quit, even though he's tired and looks like he wants to stop.

Pataki is driving himself. He is holding a lot of sadness inside, which can be seen when looking close.

Governor Pataki is determined to serve the people he represents. He believes that, with the challenges America faces, he is the best person to help address the challenges. Pataki's deeper feelings are held inside. Part of his drive today, maybe an old feeling, that he hasn't done all he could do to help others. He is a dependable person who constantly tries to address the inequities he sees in the best way he can.

What is sure is he is not a quitter and will stay in "the fight" as long as it lasts. He is in for the "long haul" and capable of follow-through where others might move on to the next challenge.

Governor Pataki is smart and quite capable when it comes to identifying issues. He is not particularly confrontational once they are identified. He will, however, stand for the ideas and values he holds dear. Pataki is a "prudent risk taker" who is better directing a fight then participating in one. He is nevertheless willing to pay the price of a position he sees as correct. He is in for the "long haul" and capable of follow-through where others might move on to the next challenge.

Pataki is a consummate politician with a long track record of serving the people of New York in many capacities. The ultimate question is, however, his lack of national recognition and limited "war chest" to fund a primary campaign leading to a nomination and a successful run for the White House.

Governor Pataki is without doubt knowledgeable. However, his delivery reveals a lack of passion and an overall feeling of sadness and despair. If passion, courage, leadership and a sense of charisma are what Americans are searching for in the next president, it is doubtful if the voters will find it in him.

CHAPTER 22

RAND PAUL

OFFICIAL PORTRAIT

"THE ANALYST"

An eye doctor with a myopic view when he looks toward Washington.

BACKGROUND INFORMATION

Current job	U.S. Senator from Kentucky, physician
Born	January 7, 1963 in Pittsburgh, PA
Religion	Presbyterian
Family	Kelley Ashby (m. 1990) Children: William, Duncan, Robert

PREVIOUS EXPERIENCE

Randal Howard Paul is the son of Carol Wells and Ron Paul, who is also a politician and physician. The elder Paul was a U.S. Representative from Texas who ran for president three times. Rand often spent summer vacations interning in his father's congressional office. The middle child of five, he grew up, as Randy, but his wife shortened it to Rand.

Paul attended Baylor University and graduated from Duke Medical School in 1988. He completed a general surgery internship at Georgia Baptist Medical Center in Atlanta, and he completed his residency in ophthalmology at Duke University Medical Center. Upon completion of his training in 1993, Dr. Paul and his wife Kelley moved to Bowling Green to start their family and begin his ophthalmology practice.

In 1995, Dr. Paul founded the Southern Kentucky Lions Eye Clinic, an organization that provides eye exams and surgery to needy families and individuals.

A large part of Dr. Paul's daily work as an ophthalmologist was dedicated to preserving the vision of seniors. During his free time, Dr. Paul performed pro-bono eye surgeries for patients across Kentucky. Additionally, he provided free eye surgery to children from around the world through his participation in the Children of the Americas Program.

On April 15, 2009, Paul gave his first political speech as a potential candidate at a Tea Party rally held in Bowling Green, Kentucky, where more than 700 people gathered in support of the Tea Party movement.

Elected to the Senate in 2010, Dr. Paul has proven to be an outspoken champion for constitutional liberties and fiscal responsibility. As a fierce advocate against government overreach, Rand has fought tirelessly to return government to its limited, constitutional scope.

On May 20, 2015, Paul spoke for 10 and a half hours in opposition to the reauthorization of Section 215 of the Patriot Act. Sections of the Patriot

Act were prevented from being reauthorized on June 1.

GOODFIELD PERSONALITY TYPING
TYPE 3.1 THE ANALYST
A feeling, thinking person who looks at himself through the eyes of others.

First Impression
- An intelligent, pleasant person
- A calculated risk-taker
- A man with intensity
- A principled, outspoken man
- Man of the people

Photo Courtesy of Gage Skidmore

Five reasons why this person is an Analyst type 3.1
1. Teary eyes (squinting)
2. One eye more open than the other
3. Tighten top lip
4. Concentration lines around and between eyes
5. Shallow breathing

Symbolic Level of Non-Verbal Leak

SL 1 - Pain

SL 2 - Anger in

SL 3 - Control by:
- distancing
- biting down

Photo Wikimedia

Non-Verbal Leak (NVL)
- Eyes open
- Teary eyes (squinting)
- One eye more open than the other

- Jaw shifting
- Building up pressure around mouth
- Tighten top lip
- Biting down
- Swallow down
- Eyes open

Unconscious Meaning of the NVL

"I feel pain and disbelief, and it makes me sad and angry. I don't want to express those feelings, so I wait, watch what you will do, and then I express my anger and swallow my sad feelings down, I put on a fake smile and seduce those around me."

PSYCHOLOGICAL OBSERVATION AND PUBLIC COMMENTS

Although outspoken, Senator Paul says 10 percent of what he really feels. He is more of a thinker of his feelings than a feeler of his feelings. He knows what he wants to say and how he wants it to be heard. In that sense he is strong, quiet and judgmental about not only himself but also others.

Paul has a high thought-per-word ratio and is not willing to waste his time with those who won't listen to him. He is reluctant to engage with those who will not listen to his well-thought-out positions. The problem is, as a politician he cannot act as a physician with skilled professional opinions that need respect and attention. His political job requires a different approach. It is a source of frustration, however, as he does not suffer fools well. He sees himself as a man of the people and is frustrated by bureaucracy. Many see Dr. Paul as their advocate, as he is compassionate toward those whom he feels are not treated fairly.

If Dr. Paul tells you something, you can trust it; he is in that sense trustworthy. He is a serious person who is open to opposing views as long as they are not too different. He is attentive, thoughtful and competent. His analytical approach to differences allows him to drill into the subject matter, often to the other person's chagrin. It helps him to be cool in a crisis.

He has a strong work ethic and a lot of energy. Standards are high for himself and others. This is a source of frustration when others fail to meet his expectations. He inwardly is condescending toward others who do not see his reality. He can intellectualize his hostility toward others who hold positions other than his own.

When Senator Paul does show humor, it is with irony. If he trusts you, he is very approachable and interested in your issues, particularly. Particularly if he sees your problems as a result of insensitive government. He is a man who intellectualizes his aggression and finds justification for giving it expression. In that sense, Washington D.C. politics are a more perfect match than practicing as an eye doctor in Kentucky.

Senator Paul is analytical and compassionate at the same time. The philosophical positions taken by his father are, of course, an obvious influence on his political viewpoints. He is carrying on the family tradition of outspoken support of the underdog who is being oppressed by an insensitive government.

Paul's positions are frustrating for those looking to him for flexibility and openness. He is a man of his word which is of course, the good news. The bad news is that his word reflects a position which is held by a political minority called the Tea Party.

Senator Paul's positions are 2.5 deviations away from the mean of the average American voter. To him this is simply proof of how much the president and the congress are out of touch with the people. He is there to put them right, and the presidency will serve this purpose well. He is absolutely consistent in that regard, as his position and approach are consistent. Don't looked to this man for rethinking his philosophy. The die is cast, and his position and approach are and ever shall be unwavering. Losing is not the issue — the good fight is!

Paul is a very intelligent man who must on some level be aware of how untenable his position is. As a man of honor and integrity, this logic and insight do not dissuade him; they simply make him try harder. He is the 2016 version of Jiminy Cricket, Pinocchio's conscience that told him to do the right thing. Unfortunately, he was a fictional Walt Disney character with a good message that seems not to resonate in these times.

Paul is the only Analyst type 3.1 running for President in 2016.

CHAPTER 23

RICK PERRY

PHOTO COURTESY OF GAGE SKIDMORE

"THE PLOTTER"

Even looking through new glasses – his boots still look dull.

BACKGROUND INFORMATION

Current job	Former Governor of Texas
Born	March 4, 1950 in Pint Creek, TX
Religion	Evangelical Christian
Family	Anita Thigpen (m. 1982) Children: Griffin, Sydney

PREVIOUS EXPERIENCE

A fifth-generation Texan, Perry grew up in Haskell County, Texas of West Texas. His parents were cotton farmers Joseph Ray Perry and Amelia June Holt. Perry's ancestry is almost entirely English, dating as far back as the original 13 colonies. His family has been in Texas since before the Texas Revolution.

Perry attended Texas A&M University, where he was a member of the Corps of Cadets and a member of the Alpha Gamma Rho fraternity. Perry graduated in 1972 with a Bachelor of Science in animal science.

In 1972 Perry was commissioned as an officer in the United States Air Force and completed pilot training in February 1974. He was then assigned as a C-130 pilot to the 772nd Tactical Airlift Squadron at Dyess Air Force Base. He left the United States Air Force in 1977 with the rank of Captain, returned to Texas, and went into business farming cotton with his father.

In 1984, Perry was elected to the Texas House of Representatives as a Democrat. On September 29, 1989, Perry announced that he was switching parties and becoming a Republican. As Agriculture Commissioner from 1991-1999, Perry was responsible for promoting the sale of Texas farm produce to other states and foreign nations, and for supervising the calibration of weights and measures such as gasoline pumps and grocery store scales.

In 1998, Perry chose not to seek a third term as Agriculture Commissioner.

He served as Lieutenant Governor of Texas from 1999 till 2000. From 2000 until 2015, he served as the 47th Governor of Texas. He was the longest-serving governor in Texas state history. During Perry's governorship, Texas rose from second to first among states with the highest proportion of uninsured residents at 26 percent, and the state had the lowest level of access to prenatal care in the U.S. Perry and the state legislature cut Medicaid spending. His spokeswoman stated, "Texas does provide an adequate safety net to those truly in need... and many individuals simply choose not to purchase healthcare coverage."

After announcing his candidacy for president in 2011, Perry immediately became a serious contender in the race. However, Perry's campaign began to suffer following a number of poor debate performances, and he quit.

GOODFIELD PERSONALITY TYPING
TYPE 1.2 THE PLOTTER
Ambivalent about being present

First Impression
- Very nice guy
- Charming toward others
- Honest character
- George Bush look-a-like
- Open but somewhat tentative
- Not forceful in conflict

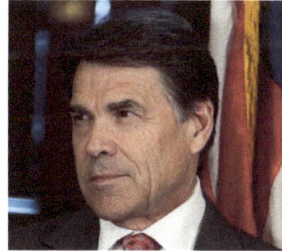

Photo Courtesy of Gage Skidmore

Five reasons why this person is a Plotter type 1.2
1. Trance, but not showing all the time
2. Eyes don't close completely
3. Eyebrows up
4. Tightness around the mouth
5. Mouth that is not completely closed

Symbolic Level of Non-Verbal Leak

SL 1 - Denial

SL 2 - Sadness

Anger
seen by cynicism

SL 3 - Control by:
- holding back
- trance

PHOTO COURTESY OF GAGE SKIDMORE

Non-Verbal Leak (NVL)
- Eyes open
- Teary partially open eyes
- Eyes close
- Biting down
- Lines bilateral nose and mouth intensified
- Tension around the mouth
- Eyebrows elevated
- Block in throat Swallow down
- Eyes open

Unconscious Meaning of the NVL
   "I am denying myself, and that makes me sad and also angry. I try not to express it. I do not trust myself expressing my feelings, and that makes me unsure."

PSYCHOLOGICAL OBSERVATION AND PUBLIC COMMENTS

Governor Perry is once again running for the presidency. He is determined to make a difference in his goal for the White House. Although Governor of Texas the 12th largest economy in the world, one does not get the feeling that Perry is a strong leader with a bold style. He does not exert the personal power that one might expect from an individual with such credentials. At times after making a powerful statement he hesitates and looks into the camera or toward the interviewer with an expression that says, "Did I say that right?"

Governor Rick Perry is a nice, open, charming, likable guy. He is clear about what he thinks is correct. Perry has a tendency to see issues in black and white. The question is not about his personal attributes but rather the ability to deliver them in a tough political environment where oratory may take a backseat to content and reason.

In a debating situation with a skilled orator with a lot of experience such as Hillary Clinton, Perry would not last long nor would the Republican aspirations to recapturing the White House. About the 2012 presidential election, he said, "I botched it."

Perry was not wearing the black horned-rim glasses we saw on him in the first Republican debate of 2011. If the goal is to come across more studious and intelligent, it's more important what comes out of his mouth than what sits on his nose. He comes across like the Rick Perry of old, trying to counter the remarks and impressions some had of him as a not-so-bright person. By holding his feelings inside, it gives the impression of anxiety and sadness.

Perry is dependable and is consistently struggling to achieve long-term objectives. He is somewhat capable of defending his views when he feels attacked. Governor Perry's be-speckled image reinforces the idea of prudence; however, some might consider it simply a reluctance to act. He is capable of deep commitment and goal- oriented behavior. He can be systematic in his approach to conflict resolution.

As much as he says powerful words at times, the nonverbal behavior of Governor Perry suggests a lack of strength in his presentation. His hesitation suggests an anxiety or uncertainty about what he is saying.

Perry comes across like a student poorly prepared for his oral presentation. He leaves one wondering are these his words or somebody else's? He hesitates and stumbles to get them out. In his heart of hearts, does he really want this job?

CHAPTER 24

MARCO RUBIO

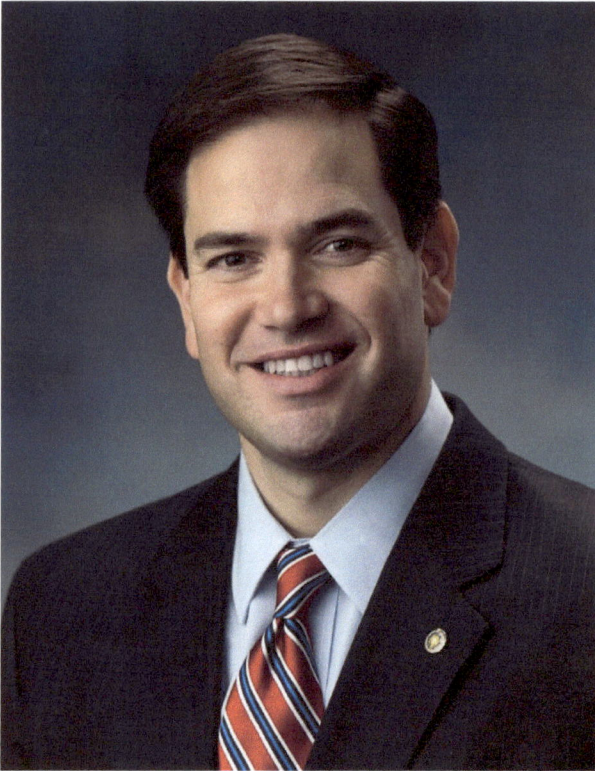

OFFICIAL PORTRAIT

"THE DOUBTER"

A meticulously grown brain hitched to one of the fastest tongues in the race.

BACKGROUND INFORMATION

Current job	U.S. Senator from Florida
Born	May 28, 1971 in Miami, FL
Religion	Roman Catholic
Family	Jeanette Dousdebes (m. 1998) Children: Amanda, Daniella, Anthony, Dominic

PREVIOUS EXPERIENCE

Marco Rubio is the son of Mario Rubio Reina and Oriales Garcia. His parents were Cubans who immigrated to the United States in 1956, prior to the rise of Fidel Castro in January 1959. His parents were naturalized in 1975. Rubio is of Spanish descent.

Rubio's family was Roman Catholic; though from age 8 to age 11, he and his family attended The Church of Jesus Christ of Latter-day Saints while living in Las Vegas. There his father worked as a bartender at Sam's Town Hotel and his mother was a housekeeper at the Imperial Palace Hotel and Casino. Rubio received his first communion as a Catholic in 1984, before moving back to Miami with his family a year later. He was confirmed and married in the Catholic Church.

In 1989, Rubio attended Tarkio College for one year on a football scholarship before enrolling at Santa Fe Community College (now Santa Fe College). He earned his Bachelor of Arts degree in political science from the University of Florida in 1993, and his J.D. degree cum laude from the University of Miami School of Law in 1996. He served as a City Commissioner for West Miami before being elected in early 2000 to the Florida House of Representatives, where he served until 2008.

In 2002, Rubio was appointed the Florida House Majority Leader. In 2006, Rubio became the first Cuban American to become Speaker of the Florida House of Representatives. In 2011, he became a U.S. Senator from Florida.

On April 13, 2015, Rubio announced his candidacy for president in 2016 and that he would not seek re-election to his Senate seat.

GOODFIELD PERSONALITY TYPING
TYPE 3 THE DOUBTER
Searching for the truth with big "T"

Photo Courtesy of Gage
Skidmore

First Impression
- Bright
- Focussed
- Convinced of his position
- Charismatic
- Informed

Five reasons why this person is the Doubter type 3
1. Eyebrows up
2. Teariness and tightening eyelids (squinting)
3. Somewhat developed jaws
4. Tongue out/in
5. Blocked breathing

Symbolic Level of Non-Verbal Leak

SL 1 - Disbelief/pain

SL 2 - Anger

SL 3 - Control by calculated emotional response

PHOTO COURTESY OF GAGE SKIDMORE

Non-Verbal Leak (NVL)
- Eyes open
- Eyebrows up
- Eyes closed
- Eyes open
- Teariness and tightening eyelids (squinting)
- Somewhat developed jaws
- Tension upper lip

116

- Pressing lips
- Blocked breathing
- Tongue out/in
- Eyes open

Unconscious Meaning of the NVL
   "When I feel pain and anger, I turn the feelings inward, and intellectualize and deny them."

PSYCHOLOGICAL OBSERVATION AND PUBLIC COMMENTS

Senator Rubio is bright, clear, powerful, strong, hard-working, orderly, focused and longing to be president of the United States. All of those characteristics lead him to see others who do not share his viewpoint as naïve, ill-informed and yes, even dangerous. He has high expectations of others and is also frustrated by others' lack of perfection and focus.

Rubio seeks symmetry and balance. When it is not there in his view, he feels frustrated. Intimacy and openness are not his strongest points. Rubio may have self-doubt, but he covers it well. He is quite comfortable in his position of power. He has a youthful, charismatic approach to issues facing America. To Rubio at this time in history, failure is most attributable to a failure of leadership by those currently in power. This is a mistake, he assures those who will listen to him, that he will not make. What drives him to run for the White House is an unwavering conviction that he has the answers. He must and can address these ills afflicting the United States. He is absolutely convinced of his abilities to restore America to "greatness again."

Senator Rubio radiates a kind of determined sadness, one that takes pain and turns it into action. It is also one that turns his perception into a viable plan for change.

He shows great compassion, one that reflexes his own family's struggle for survival building from little to a life of substance. He is the quintessential example of the American Dream come true. Rubio's awareness of his roots gives him a connection with many Americans still suffering and striving to make their own American Dream a reality.

Rubio will clearly never forget his origins; that is not the question. The question is, can the drive in him be communicated to a large enough American public bombarded by promises and hyperbole? Can they hear a voice with whom they can trust and identify?

Rubio has the power, the patience, and even the plan! What stands between him and the White House are endurance, attention, believability, and enough voters who see him vanish from a Mad Hatter's Tea Party.

Will that happen? It depends on how much he wants to become president of the United States.

CHAPTER 25

BERNIE SANDERS

OFFICIAL PORTRAIT

"THE DOUBTER"

A person who's as far left as can be and still be called a Democrat.

BACKGROUND INFORMATION

Current job	U.S. Senator from Vermont
Born	September 8, 1941 in Brooklyn, NY
Religion	Jewish
Family	Deborah Shiling (m. 1964-1966), Jane O'Meara Driscoll (m. 1988) Children: Levi (with Susan Mott), 3 stepchildren

PREVIOUS EXPERIENCE

Bernie Sanders is the son of Eli Sanders and Dorothy Glassberg. His father was a Jewish immigrant from Poland whose family was killed in the Holocaust, while his mother was born to Jewish parents in New York City.

Sanders has said that he became interested in politics at an early age: "A guy named Adolf Hitler won an election in 1932 ... and 50 million people died as a result ... what I learned as a little kid is that politics is, in fact, very important."

Sanders went to Brooklyn College for a year before transferring to the University of Chicago. While at the university, Sanders was active in the Civil Rights Movement and was a student organizer for the Congress of Racial Equality and the Student Nonviolent Coordinating Committee. In 1964, Sanders graduated from the University of Chicago with a BA degree in political science.

Sanders began his political career in 1971 as a member of the Liberty Union Party, which originated in the anti-war and people's party movement. After unsuccessful candidacies to be Vermont's governor and a U.S. Senator, Sanders was elected Mayor of Burlington, Vermont's most populous city, in 1981. He was reelected to three more two-year mayoral terms before being elected to represent Vermont's at-large congressional district in the United States House of Representatives in 1990. He served as a congressman for 16 years before being elected to succeed the retiring Republican-turned-independent Jim Jeffords in the U.S. Senate in 2006. In 2012, he was reelected by a large margin, capturing almost 71 percent of the popular vote.

Sanders is the longest-serving Independent in U.S. congressional history. A self-described democratic socialist, he favors policies similar to those of social democratic parties in Europe, particularly those of Scandinavia. He caucuses with the Democratic Party and has been the ranking minority member on the Senate Budget Committee since January 2015.

Since his election to the Senate, Sanders has emerged as a leading progressive voice on issues like income inequality, climate change, and campaign finance reform. He rose to national prominence on the heels of his 2010 filibuster of the proposed extension of the Bush-era tax rates for the wealthy. Sanders is also outspoken on civil liberties issues, and he has been particularly critical of mass surveillance policies such as the Patriot Act.

GOODFIELD PERSONALITY TYPING
TYPE 3 THE DOUBTER
Searching for the truth with big "T"

First Impression
- Tough
- Rigid
- Long history fighting injustice
- Angry man about injustice
- Tough old bird
- Always fighting something
- The hero of the underdog
- Smart but unrealistic

Photo Courtesy of Gage Skidmore

Five reasons why this person is the Doubter type 3
1. Eyebrows up
2. Teariness and tightening eyelids (squinting)
3. Somewhat developed jaws
4. Tongue out/in
5. Blocked breathing

Non-Verbal Leak (NVL)

- Eyes open
- Eyebrows up
- Eyes closed
- Eyes open
- Teariness and tightening eyelids (squinting)
- Somewhat developed jaws
- Tension upper lip
- Pressing lips
- Blocked breathing
- Tongue out/in
- Eyes open

Unconscious Meaning of the NVL

"I am in pain, I don't belief what happened to me. I am angry and sad. I'm not authorized to express it, so I control it by holding in and intellectualize."

PSYCHOLOGICAL OBSERVATION AND PUBLIC COMMENTS

Senator Sanders is bright and powerful, possessing an extremely rigid ego. He has high expectations of himself and others, which constantly serve as both a source of frustration and inspiration for his hard work and private crusade. He feels the pressure to share his message while, at the same time, having a little insight (at least not shared publicly) as to its causality. He is outspoken; but for those who look closer, he is holding his cards close to his chest. Sanders is frequently misunderstood and therefore written off by those who might appreciate his message if they could overlook his delivery style.

Sanders is a keen observer, full of faults and frailty, who has difficulties in relationships with those who are not dazzled by "the light" of his radiant insights.

On some level he has a fear of rejection. Sanders often successfully masks this with left-wing hyperbole and dismissive remarks of others. He revels in his newly acquired leadership position, brandishing his own brand of home-spun charisma.

Senator Sanders is an idealist in the same way that Don Quixote was. He fights the "good fight." He knows his chances are slim to none, but it never deters him. He is both loved and laughed at by pragmatic politicians. He fights for what he sees as right against that which is realistic. His battle-scarred logic has allowed him to literally be a voice in the wilderness, arguing moral causes as he sees them. He is a moral curmudgeon, holding a mirror up to those who perpetuate moral injustice upon the masses.

Senator Sanders' candidacy for the presidency, although completely unrealistic, serves a purpose. He encourages the American people to look at inequities and injustice perpetrated by those in power and by those seeking to maintain power. Sanders is the voice of the little man or woman whose needs have been trampled upon and discounted. He certainly is a person who has been fighting the perceived injustice in his own life for years and now has an opportunity to project those inequities onto the political scene.

Sanders' candidacy and left-wing socialist philosophy stands as a reminder that the underdog, although assured to lose, should not be forgotten in the ever-growing big picture of the 2016 American rush toward political victory.

Sanders is like Howard Beale from Paddy Chayefsky's movie "Network." Sanders is passionate, wild, outspoken, and some say "unrealistic and crazy." To some, he is a "summer anomaly" blown in from the left. To others, he is a political "Elmer Gantry" spouting his brand of truth to whomever listens. More and more people are trying to get into the tent to hear his political fire-and-brimstone message.

Sanders is probably a bug on the windshield of Hillary Clinton's juggernaut.

CHAPTER 26

RICK SANTORUM

PHOTO COURTESY OF GAGE SKIDMORE

"THE THINKER"

A bright, serious man, needing a major humor transplant.

BACKGROUND INFORMATION

Current job	Attorney
Born	May 10, 1958 in Winchester, VA
Religion	Roman Catholic
Family	Karen Garver (m. 1990)
	Children Gabriel (†) Elizabeth, Richard, Daniel, Sarah, Peter, Patrick, Isabella

PREVIOUS EXPERIENCE

Santorum is the son of Aldo Santorum, a clinical psychologist who immigrated to the United States at age seven from Riva del Garda, Italy, and Catherine Dughi, an administrative nurse who is of Italian and Irish ancestry.

Santorum grew up in Virginia and Pennsylvania, his family lived in an apartment provided by the Veterans Administration. Santorum attended Butler Senior High School and was nicknamed "Rooster," supposedly for both a cowlick strand of hair and an assertive nature, particularly on important political issues. After his parents transferred to the Naval Station Great Lakes in northern Illinois, Santorum attended the Roman Catholic Carmel High School in Mundelein, Illinois, for one year, graduating in 1976.

Santorum attended Pennsylvania State University for his undergraduate studies, serving as chairman of the university's College Republicans chapter and graduating with a BA degree with honors in political science in 1980. He completed a one-year MBA program at the University of Pittsburgh's Joseph M. Katz Graduate School of Business, graduating in 1981. In 1986, Santorum received a JD degree with honors from Dickinson School of Law.

After graduating, Santorum was admitted to the Pennsylvania bar and practiced law for four years at the Pittsburgh law firm Kirkpatrick & Lockhart. Santorum left his private law practice in 1990 after his election to the House of Representatives.

From 1995-2007, Santorum served in the U.S. Senate representing Pennsylvania.

After Senator Santorum's election to the Senate, he sought to "practice what [he] preached" and hired five people for his staff who were on welfare, food stamps, or other government aid.

In January 2007, Santorum joined the Ethics and Public Policy Center, a D.C.-based conservative think tank, as director of its America's Enemies Program, focusing on foreign threats to the United States, including Islamic fascism, Venezuela, North Korea and Russia. In February 2007, he signed a deal to become a contributor on the Fox News Channel, offering commentary on politics and public policy. In March 2007, he joined Eckert Seamans, where he primarily practiced law in the firm's Pittsburgh and Washington, D.C., offices, providing business and strategic counseling services to the firm's clients. In 2007, he joined the Board of Directors of Universal Health Services, a hospital management company based in King of Prussia, Pennsylvania. He also began writing an Op/Ed column, "The Elephant in the Room", for *The Philadelphia Inquirer*.

Santorum ran for the 2012 Republican presidential nomination, and won 11 state primaries and received nearly 4 million votes. Ultimately, he suspended his campaign after his eighth child, Isabella, was in an extended hospitalization. She suffered from Edwards Syndrome (Trisomy 18), a genetic disorder that has only a 10 percent chance of survival past one year of age.

GOODFIELD PERSONALITY TYPING
Type 2.1 THE THINKER
Pensive thinker of feelings

First Impression

- Intelligent
- No humor
- Focussed
- True believer
- Informed
- Tick-skinned
- Passive-aggressive regarding expression of anger

Photo Courtesy of Gage Skidmore

Five reasons why this person is a Thinker Type 2.1

1. Eyes wide open with shock and old tears in one eye
2. Concentration lines
3. Developed Masseter
4. Tension around mouth
5. Jaw shifts

126

Symbolic Level of Non-Verbal Leak

SL 1 - Shock/pain
SL 2 - Anger/sadness
SL 3 - Control by:
- distancing
- swallowing down

PHOTO COURTESY OF GAGE SKIDMORE

Non-Verbal Leak (NVL)
- Eyes open
- One eye shock
- One eye shows tears
- Concentration lines Eyes closed
- Developed masseter
- Tension around mouth
- Jaw shifts
- Swallowing down
- Eyes open

Unconscious Meaning of the NVL

"I have pain and I am angry and sad. I cannot show it so I keep it inside. I swallow it down, and I will find a hole in your logic and let it out then on you."

PSYCHOLOGICAL OBSERVATION AND PUBLIC COMMENTS

Santorum is a man of intelligence, character, honesty, and integrity. He is loyal and trustworthy and somewhat open to change, if it is argued in a very logical way. His tentative style is that of a prudent approach that makes him attractive to his conservative constituency.

What he lacks in humor he makes up for with logic. He works hard at being soft and warm. He is affable and is not afraid to take a moral stance on controversial issues.

Senator Santorum is a thinker of feelings, *not* a feeler of feelings. He says all the right words but without much affect. He has the capacity to inspire, not with his passion but with his logic. He is a calculated risk-taker, evaluating events carefully before taking action. He has the capacity to offer sound advice and counsel on complex issues.

Santorum is a quick study of people. He is a quiet fighter, using intellect, logic and rhetoric to support and defend his viewpoints which are often seen as controversial. His verbal skills make him a natural mediator and negotiator.

Senator Santorum revels in controversy and is often seen as an agent provocateur. This perception, often held by others, fits his self-concept well. He is a straight-shooter whose gun shoots toward the right. Santorum's somewhat rigid thinking, and reluctance to acknowledge the possibility that others might be correct in their thinking, make him vulnerable to people with strong logic and convincing information as well.

There is no doubt about Senator Santorum's willingness to defend his arguments regardless of the consequences. He is, however, limited to openness toward difference. This close-mindedness has helped to hone him into a formidable opponent, with his right-or-wrong approach to difference when his views and values are challenged.

Santorum is a polished package well organized but may be in need of a humor transplant.

Santorum is the only Thinker type 2.1 running for President in 2016.

CHAPTER 27

DONALD TRUMP

PHOTO COURTESY OF GAGE SKIDMORE

"THE POUNCER"

A "Wild Hair" in the Republican's caucus.

BACKGROUND INFORMATION

Current job	Real estate developer, television personality
Born	June 14, 1946 in Queens, NY
Religion	Presbyterian
Family	Ivana Zelníčková (m. 1977–1992) Marla Maples (m. 1993–1999) Melania Knauss-Trump (m. 2005) Children: Donald, Ivanka, Eric, Tiffany, Barron

PREVIOUS EXPERIENCE

Donald Trump is the son of Mary Anne MacLeod and Fred Trump. Trump's mother was a Scottish immigrant, born on the Isle of Lewis, off the west coast of Scotland. Trump's paternal grandparents were German immigrants; Trump's grandfather, Friedrich Drumpf, was a successful Klondike Gold Rush restaurateur who anglicized the family name.

Trump attended the private Kew-Forest School in Forest Hills, Queens, where Fred Trump, Donald's father, was a member of the Board of Trustees. Trump's father told an interviewer in 1983 his son "was a pretty rough fellow when he was small," prompting him to enroll his son in the New York Military Academy (NYMA) in eighth grade for the duration of his high school education. Trump participated in marching drills and wore a uniform, attaining the rank of "cadet captain" in his senior year.

Trump attended Wharton School of the University of Pennsylvania, because Wharton then had one of the few real estate studies departments in U.S. He graduated in 1968, with a Bachelor of Science degree in economics.

Trump began his career at his father's real estate company, Elizabeth Trump and Son. In 1971, Trump moved to Manhattan and became involved in larger building projects, using attractive architectural design to win public recognition. He later created The Trump Organization. Beyond his traditional ventures in real estate and the hospitality and entertainment industries, Trump has established the Trump name and brand in other industries and products with mixed success. The Trump Organization operates many golf courses and resorts in the United States and around the world.

Over the course of his career, Trump has initiated and been the target of "hundreds" of civil lawsuits, which Trump lawyer Alan Garten said in 2015 was "a natural part of doing business in this country." Four of Trump's businesses have declared Chapter 11 bankruptcy.

A 2011 report by the Center for Responsive Politics showed that over two decades of U.S. elections, Donald Trump made contributions to campaigns of both Republican and Democratic Party candidates.

Trump spent over $1 million to research a possible to run for president of the United States. In October 2013, New York Republicans had circulated a memo suggesting Trump should run for governor of the state in 2014, against Andrew Cuomo. Trump said that while New York had problems and taxes were too high, running for governor was not of great interest to him. In 2015, Trump announced to run for president of the United States in the 2016 election. He announced to use his own money and doesn't want a salary when he is the U.S. president.

GOODFIELD PERSONALITY TYPING
TYPE 2.3 THE POUNCER
Danger on two feet

First Impression
- Bombastic and overwhelming
- Outspoken and opinionated
- A force to be reckoned with
- Street smart
- Believes most of his BS
- Victory at all cost, including reason
- Charismatic
- The definition of the word arrogant

Photo Courtesy of Gage Skidmore

Five reasons why this person is the Pouncer type 2.3
1. Shock showing somewhat in eyes
2. Shifting of jaws
3. Tight top lip
4. Eyebrows pulled together (furrowed)
5. Block in throat

Non-Verbal Leak (NVL)

- Shock showing somewhat in eyes
- Shifting of jaws
- Tight top lip
- Eyebrows pulled together (furrowed)Tighten top lip
- Swallow down
- Eyes open

Unconscious Meaning of the NVL

   "I am shocked and want to express my anger. Instead I hold it inside until I can find the correct opportunity to express it fully."

PSYCHOLOGICAL OBSERVATION AND PUBLIC COMMENTS

Donald Trump is often found at the center of the fray when action is required. He has a knack for knowing what is necessary to obtain his objectives. He is a skilled observer of others' actions and steps in when decisive action is necessary. He is skilled at reducing the dynamics of a situation. He will not hesitate to speak up when the time is "right"- and even sometimes when the time is not right.

Trump always has his eyes open for those people who are on the inside and those people who aren't. He loves being the center of attention and showing his power, skills, and riches.

Trump is a little boy who wants to prove to the world he is strong. This behavior is a way of avoiding deeper anxieties that he may or may not have addressed. He is a person capable of rationalizing his actions after setting his goals. As much as he says he loves women, he has difficulty with really trusting them on a deep level. He is a passionate man who on some level denies his deeper feelings. When it comes to family and friends, he is 100 percent loyal.

Trump has an object relationship with people in general. Many are seen as players on *his* chessboard, never on their own. If you're in with "The Donald," then you are really in for an adventure that may be mutually advantageous.

The basic issue with Donald Trump is a deep distrust of anything or anybody. It is an unconscious struggle to prove he is invincible to the world. He believes he is both bright and lucky. He will not knowingly hire a person who sees the world differently than he does, as that person would threaten his unconscious self-concept.

Trump is approaching this election as one might expect, as a business deal to be negotiated and manipulated to final success or victory. Those who fail to realize this do so at their own peril. When it comes to hardball negotiations, Donald Trump makes Vladimir Putin look like a frightened naïve amateur. Welcome to the wonderful world of Trump!

Donald Trump is, if nothing else, a great real estate salesman. The property for which he is negotiating is the United States and the rest of the world. This being his biggest potential acquisition, one would do well to study some of his books. In the "The Art of the Deal," he says "I like thinking big. I always have. To me it's very simple: if you're going to be thinking anyway, you might as well think big." The titles "Time to Get Tough: Making America #1 Again" and "Think Like a Champion: An Informal Education in Business and Life" say it all.

Regardless of how you might feel about him, underneath that bizarre coiffured hair lurks a large brain, connected to a strong backbone that will not go away.

Don't count him out just yet! "The Donald" may "duck" but he won't quit.

CHAPTER 28

SCOTT WALKER

PHOTO COURTESY OF GAGE SKIDMORE

"THE DOUBTER"

A top mid-level executive dreaming of becoming the Chief Executive.

BACKGROUND INFORMATION

Current job	Governor of Wisconsin
Born	November 2, 1967 in Colorado Springs, CO
Religion	Evangelical Christian
Family	Tonette Tarantino (m. 1993) Children: Matt, Alex

PREVIOUS EXPERIENCE

Scott Walker is the son of Patricia Ann Fitch, a bookkeeper, and Llewellyn Scott Walker, a Baptist minister. In high school, Walker attended two weeks of American Legion-sponsored training in leadership and government at Badger Boys State in Wisconsin and the selective Boys Nation in Washington, D.C. Walker has credited the experience with solidifying his interest in public service and giving him the "political bug." He attained the highest rank, Eagle Scout, in the Boy Scouts of America.

In 1986, Walker enrolled at Marquette University. Walker discontinued his studies at Marquette in the spring of 1990. He earned 94 of the 128 minimum credits needed to graduate. He left in good standing but without obtaining a degree. Walker has said he dropped out of college when he received an offer for a full-time job with the American Red Cross. He had worked part-time in college for IBM selling warranties on mainframe computers, which led to the American Red Cross position.

Walker was elected to the Wisconsin State Assembly in 1992, representing a district in western Milwaukee County. In 2002, Walker was elected County Executive in a special election following the resignation of F. Thomas Ament. He was elected for a full term in 2004 and was reelected in 2008.

Shortly after his inauguration in 2011 as the Governor of Wisconsin, Walker introduced a budget plan which limited the collective bargaining abilities of most Wisconsin public employees. The state's $3.6 billion budget deficit was turned into a surplus and taxes were cut by $2 billion. More than 100,000 jobs were created in the state of Wisconsin. However, the state has yet to regain all the jobs lost during and after the Great Recession of 2007–2009. The response to Walker's policies included protests at the Wisconsin State Capitol and an effort to recall Walker. In 2012, Walker become the first American governor to survive a recall effort.

GOODFIELD PERSONALITY TYPING
TYPE 3 THE DOUBTER
Searching for the truth with big "T"

First Impression
- Salesman
- True believer
- Convinced of his position
- Charismatic
- Informed

Photo Courtesy of Gage
Skidmore

Five reasons why this person is the Doubter type 3
1. Eyebrows up
2. Teariness and tightening eyelids (squinting)
3. Somewhat developed jaws
4. Tongue out/in
5. Blocked breathing

Symbolic Level of Non-Verbal Leak

SL 1 - Disbelief/pain

SL 2 - Anger

SL 3 - Control by calculated emotional response

Non-Verbal Leak (NVL)
- Eyes open
- Eyebrows up
- Eyes closed
- Eyes open
- Teariness and tightening eyelids (squinting)
- Somewhat developed jaws
- Tension upper lip

- Pressing lips
- Blocked breathing
- Tongue out/in
- Eyes open

Unconscious Meaning of the NVL
    "I feel the pain, and I don't belief what happened to me. I am angry. I'm not authorized to express it so I control it by holding in."

PSYCHOLOGICAL OBSERVATION AND PUBLIC COMMENTS

Governor Walker is a very hard-working nice guy who wants better for himself, family, state and country. He is a natural salesman and fighter for middle class values and ways.

Walker has strong religious convictions and is a true believer. He comes across like a top mid-level executive. Walker is a fighter who is powerful, stubborn, and bright, with a rigid ego and a will to fight for that what he believes. He has high expectations of himself and others and is frustrated when others do not live up to his standards.

Governor Walker is very much a family man who wants intimacy but has difficulty with intimacy. He is an excellent judge of character. Beneath that self-assured exterior is a person with self-doubt and some insecurities. This is charisma with the small "c" instead of a capital "C."

Governor Walker's fear of failure on a very deep level is the catalyst for his strong and somewhat rigid attitudes and positions. He has demonstrated a great capacity for leadership under pressure. There are many who admire him for this capacity and his willingness to forestall immediate gratification. He will fight for his brand of "right" in the future.

Walker's position supports "marriage between one man and one woman." He cut off state funding for abortion providers. If you add that to his somewhat rigid and dogmatic approach to differences, it would seem safe to say that his chances to receive his party's nomination are a challenge — one that will test his communication skills, philosophy and political acumen as well as the basic core values of the Republican Party.

Walker is not a quitter nor someone willing to compromise his values. What to many may be his strength, may prove to be his party's weakness. If they adopt his principal position, they have to sell it to the American voters.

Scott Walker has a plan and is determined to reach his goals. The major question is can he successfully communicate his vision to a very large group of people? His rigid ego structure and his semi-charismatic style lead others to believe he has the power, path, and persistence to reach his goals. His pressure to succeed is readily transmitted to others.

Walker has high expectations of himself that may be unrealistic given the long journey to the White House. With all the people running and all the bluster and bravado, it won't be easy for a nice, middle-class man to raise his voice above a bunch of vehement, vocal, vitriolic would-be victors.

CHAPTER 29

JIM WEBB

OFFICIAL PORTRAIT

"THE DOER"

A genuine combat hero showing anxiety in his White House battle.

BACKGROUND INFORMATION

Current job	Author
Born	February 9, 1946 in St. Joseph, MO
Religion	Christian
Family	Barbara Samorajczyk (m. 1968-1979)
	Jo Ann Krukar (m. 1981-2004)
	Hong Le Webb (m. 2005)
	Children: Amy, Sarah, Jimmy, Julia, Georgia, Emily (stepdaughter)

PREVIOUS EXPERIENCE

Webb was the son of James Henry Webb, and his wife, Vera Lorraine Hodges. He grew up in a military family, moving frequently as his father's career in the United States Air Force required. Webb is descended from Scotch-Irish immigrants from Ulster who emigrated in the mid-18th century to the British North American colonies.

Webb attended more than a dozen schools across the U.S. and in England. He attended the University of Southern California on a Navy Reserve Officer Training Corps scholarship. In 1964, Webb earned an appointment to the United States Naval Academy in Annapolis, Maryland. At Annapolis, Webb was a member of the Brigade Honor Committee and the Brigade Staff. When he graduated in 1968, he received the Superintendent's Letter for Outstanding Leadership. He was promoted to first lieutenant in the second half of his tour in Vietnam.

He served as a platoon commander with Delta Company, 1st Battalion 5th Marines. He was awarded the Navy Cross for heroism in Vietnam, the Silver Star, two Bronze Stars, and two Purple Hearts. His war wounds left him with shrapnel in his knee, kidney, and head. The injury to his knee led to a medical board that decided on medical retirement. After his medical retirement from the Marine Corps, Webb enrolled in law school at Georgetown University, where he earned a Juris Doctor and received the Horan Award for excellence in legal writing.

From 1977 to 1981, Webb worked on the staff of the House Committee on Veterans Affairs. During this time, he also represented veterans pro bono and taught at the Naval Academy. From 1984 until 1987, he was the Assistant Secretary of Defense for Reserve Affairs. From 1987 until 1988, he served as U.S. Secretary of the Navy, becoming the first Naval Academy graduate to serve as the civilian head of the Navy. From 2007 until 2013, he served as the U.S. Senator from Virginia.

Webb is a prolific writer and has written for many national journals. He wrote 10 books, and a story for the 2000 movie, "Rules of Engagement." Warner Brothers acquired Webb's script for "Wiskey River."

GOODFIELD PERSONALITY TYPING
TYPE 2 THE DOER
Boundary Checker

First Impression
- Hesitant
- Unsure of himself
- Fearful on some level
- Intelligent and reluctant
- Informed
- Personable

Photo Courtesy of Gage Skidmore

Five reasons why this person is a Doer type 2
1. Eyes wide open
2. Very pronounced jaws
3. Tongue out
4. Pressured defiant appearance
5. Tension in shoulders

Symbolic Level of Non-Verbal Leak

SL 1 - Shock/fear

SL 2 - Anger out

SL 3 - Control by:
- holding in
- denial

PHOTO COURTESY OF GAGE SKIDMORE

141

Non-Verbal Leak (NVL)
- Eyes open
- Eyes wide open
- Pronounced jaws sometimes pulsing
- Tongue in/out quick
- Tightening of the mouth
- High breathing
- Lines throat deeper
- Concentration lines stronger
- Movement of the shoulders
- Eyes close not completely (one eye more than the other)
- Eyes open

Unconscious Meaning of the NVL
"I feel unnoticed, and that makes me angry. I try not to express it, so I swallow those feelings down, until they come out later. And they really do!"

PSYCHOLOGICAL OBSERVATION AND PUBLIC COMMENTS

Senator Webb has had a distinguished career, serving America from the battlefront in Vietnam to the floor of the United States Senate. Paradoxically, somehow a close look at him leaves the impression of somebody who is sincere, hesitant and not sure of himself and his actions. He says the right things, but his nonverbal presentation shows his anxiety on some level.

Webb has been a fighting marine; but in terms of the race for the White House, it is highly doubtful that he will become a successful combatant to win 1600 Pennsylvania Ave.

Senator Webb is a person who is regularly testing himself, except on some level he comes across like he does not pass that test, according to his own standards. He is the paradox in that sense. He is clearly an extraordinarily accomplished person; nevertheless, his uncertainty permeates his presentation. It does seem however, that if there is anyone who doubts Jim Webb, it is Jim Webb himself.

Senator Webb is analytical and able to adapt to the challenges facing America. He is a very principled man, whose principles get in the way of expediency. Remember that he resigned as Secretary of the Navy over a policy he couldn't morally support.

Web is a genuine intellectual, an expert on people and their needs, a natural teacher, and an excellent salesman of his own ideas of right and wrong. Honor and integrity are his priorities. He is personable and informed. It seems like he's hiding something. To Senator Webb, action is more of a priority than intimacy. Contact and intimacy are not his strongest cards. He harbors a lot of anger, but he's not quick to express it. Webb carries a lot of pressure in his system — it shows in his jaws and top lip.

Senator Webb has the courage to stand up to Hillary Clinton, but the question is not one of courage but of good judgment. Based on his presentations about his candidacy, and the lackluster presentation of himself, there is little chance he could even make it to the floor of the Democratic Convention. He would make it as an honored guest, but perhaps he would do best sticking to his writing and leaving the dirty tactics to those who are willing to use them.

CHAPTER 30

UNCONSCIOUS REASONS

It seems to me that a person deciding to run for the highest executive office in the land probably has a deep-seated unconscious motivation to think that he or she is worthy, entitled, and destined to become the president. Thank God we have had some people who have the drive and desire. Perhaps those who would be president in the past did it for the same reasons.

The scrutiny, pressures and current realities are different, presenting new challenges and increased expectations. No secrets go undiscovered, especially with all of the latest technology allowing us to delve into the past of everyone and discover everything. They can be true or not! E-mails, indiscretions, indecisiveness — all are fodder for the press.

The juicier the item the greater the chance it will end up on the front page or the lead story on the evening news. Sexual indiscretions or questionable conduct all become "proof" of character forcing good men and women to deprive America of their skills and abilities. The media endeavors to make the public see you through your dumbest act.

The facts that context determines meaning, and perception determines reality, is forgotten or simply ignored as headlines eat people and their careers. Would you like someone going through your psychological wastebasket or garbage can? This is not to mention the grueling and outrageously expensive requirements for any successful or potentially successful campaign. Television and social media have changed the political landscape for the candidates.

You need the skills of a seasoned economist, the tactical abilities of an accomplished military strategist, and the media savvy of a successful television or film star. Former presidents like Calvin (*Silent Cal*) Coolidge, Warren G. (*Shall we play poker all day*) Harding, and William Howard (*Get help! I'm stuck in the White House bathtub*) Taft, need not consider running in 2016!

As of September 10, 2015 there are 26 people who have announced their intension or are seriously considering the possibility of entering the race for the 2016 election. I think we can divide them roughly into six camps.

CHAPTER 31

CATEGORY DESCRIPTION

THE NO (NOBLESSE OBLIGE)
Jeb Bush, Lincoln Chafee, Hillary Clinton and Rand Paul

When the circle in which you live or the family from where you come permeates your personality with a strong identity and oftentimes influences the avocation you choose.

Sometimes it seems like it is inevitable, as social pressures and public images push people toward fulfilling an expectation. Here, the names of Clinton and Bush come to mind. The same can be said of Rand Paul following in his father's footsteps.

While at Yale Law School, Hillary Rodham and Bill Clinton were both surrounded by some presidential buzz. Of course, it was more around Bill; but, Hillary was clearly in the game as well. In both of their cases, it probably related to the idea that they had better ideas for America. Proven success led to a legacy, and by many, an expectation that people wanted more Clinton, regardless of the ethics, policies and behavior. It is and was a "fit" with America. There are many who believe it still is and will continue to be. Sometimes on a deeper level we find people trying to vindicate the actions or failed actions of their parents or ancestors.

Winston Churchill is a good example of this struggle to not just walk in the footsteps of his father but also to clean up the messes that his father made during that sometimes staggering walk through history. It was also motivated by the hundreds years of heritage and expectations as a Churchill.

That is not to say that if Hilary Clinton had no specific tie to a profession, she wouldn't enter it any more than if she had a connection. The unconscious motivations are the driving forces that fit this category.

In the case of Lincoln Chafee, he fits reasonably well into the NO group, with some of his bizarre beliefs and strange voting habits. His father was a prominent United States senator who passed away during his term. The Governor of Rhode Island appointed Chafee to fill out his father's remaining term. He was later re-elected. He is a "pleaser" who wants everybody to know he's a "good guy" and to subsequently like him. The

White House, of course, would be the ultimate proof that he made it to the top. That is something even his dad did not do.

THE M&M (MESSIANIC MESSENGER)
Ben Carson and Mike Huckabee

When on a deep level within yourself you are convinced that you are being "guided" to and through a course of action, and that on some level you are just the messenger for that course, then it is easy to survive hardship, judgment, and ill will as you march forward to fulfill your destiny. The author Eric Hoffer referred to these people as "true believers."

Their spiritual background and belief system is a profound source of fortification against those who do not see the world as they do. Individuals in this category are reared in controversy, giving them an insulation from the judgmental slings and arrows of others.

Any level of defeat is simply seen as a setback and a test of their faith and character. The judgment of others is "proof" that they are in the right battle for what they believe to be the right reason, and it is only time and tenacity that will vindicate the preordained outcome.

Mike Huckabee's volunteering to go to jail for Kim Davis is an excellent example of the "M&M" philosophy in full bloom and righteousness. This was over Kim Davis' refusal to issue marriage licenses to gay couples in Kentucky due to her religious beliefs.

Ben Carson, in his book, "Think big: unleashing your potential for excellence," says "God cares about every area of our lives, and God wants us to ask for help."

The message is clear — ask Him for help, but remember who told you to do that when it comes voting time! Carson is a Christian who stirs more controversy as he utters remarks like he said on "Meet the Press" on August 16, 2015, "I would not advocate that we put a Muslim in charge of this nation." He may be a great surgeon, but his political skills could use some honing.

Carson's initial approach to a problem will be fundamentally different then, for example Chris Christie's. Carson will find it more comfortable to ponder, analyze, and reflect on the underlying dynamics of the issue. Christie may find it more comfortable to take direct action, and adjust to the needs and the demands of the situation later.

Neither difference is wrong in terms of approach. Depending on the crisis you may prefer one over the other as a successful strategy.

THE 3 "F" (FANTASIES – FRUSTRATION – FURY)
Bob Ehrlich, Bobby Jindal, Mark Rubio, Bernie Sanders, Rick Santorum, Scott Walker

These individuals march to the sound of a different drummer. There's nothing wrong with them; they simply don't see things the way many people do. Denial of others' viewpoints or input on different political issues or world views is a key factor for membership in the 3 "F" group. There is no doubt that anyone considering going through an arduous process like a presidential run must have a strong ego.

The protection of that "strong ego" from external attack is denial, distortion, and projection.

Some people might call these 3 Fers close-minded. To others they might be seen as prophets with a practical plan to resolve society's ills. However others see these individuals, as strong alternatives to the inequities suffered by our society. They are the alternatives to perceived injustice. These 3 Fers are angered with organization frustration, and they have a plan and formula that will fix what they see as wrong, unjust and unacceptable. These individuals have "rhino skin" when it comes to dealing with negative feedback and unpleasant remarks about themselves, their character, their intelligence, and in general their *"Weltanschauung"* or world view.

THE PPS (POWER PLAYERS)
Chris Christie, Hillary Clinton, Donald Trump

The power player is convinced that victory is a decision made prior to winning and therefore, failure is seen as a tactical error or failure of commitment or will power. The problem with this approach is that sometimes the "PPer" becomes dogmatic when focus is lost. It can be said that a fanatic is a person who loses the focus on the goal and redoubles their effort. It is not impossible to find this type of individual making irrational, unrealistic, and overstated remarks about his/her adversary in terms of character and integrity. They sometimes find it hard to believe they just plain got beaten by somebody who did their job better, or simply out-foxed them.

Donald Trump is not just a "power player," he believes he is the definitive definition of "power player." He is convinced that he is ultimately irresistible. "All of the women on 'The Apprentice' flirted with me — consciously or unconsciously. That's to be expected."

"The Donald" is an obvious paradox, claiming that, "It's always good to be underestimated." This remark comes from a guy who paints, prints, engraves, scrolls and plasters the name TRUMP on everything! Some may say that this conspicuous behavior is just his outspoken style, and is proof of someone with a deep inferiority complex. Others might find this "self-tagging" behavior as proof that he is strong, capable and absolutely secure about who he is - and wants the world to know it! If that's true, he hides it in plain sight on the sides of buildings and in the minds of many.

The question becomes how dangerous is a person who has to prove something when he is the most powerful person on the planet? If he lowers his shields, we may very well see the good will and compassion he has buried in his monogrammed self-concept. No one doubts that he is strong. He will not back down from a fight. "The Donald" may "duck," but he won't run.

Hillary Clinton appeared in the NO or Noblesse Oblige category. It is also quite obvious that she is an extraordinary power player. She therefore will be given additional attention in this section.

The Clinton dynasty has obviously been a power base in Washington for years. But there's a reason for that, especially when speaking of Hillary Clinton. As a person, she is focused, driven, and determined, not to mention the fact she's one of the most intelligent people in the whole race for the White House. That makes her a "power player." Of this there is no doubt. Some people don't like her style; moreover, some don't trust her. She is clearly no one to underestimate. She is a fighter who won't go away or give up. About this she says, "You don't walk away if you love someone. You help the person." The other thing you can do is just to make a deal with them.

Chris Christie is a New Jersey street-wise person. As a former federal prosecutor, he didn't make a lot of friends with some of his actions. That never deterred him. He is out to do a job and is ready to fight at anytime. Inside this man is a working- class person who is serious about doing his job the best way he can. There's nothing sophisticated or complicated about his actions. What you see is what you get.

Christie a quick-thinker and just as quickly makes a judgment about individuals and events. He intuitively knows who is with him or who is against him. He is not a person who sits down and philosophically reviews his past decisions. He is concerned about obstacles and those who created them on the way to his goal. It's been said a lot, but what you see is what you get!

THE OTP (THE ONE TRICK PONY)
Mark Everson and Rick Perry

These people are the psychological party crashers. These are people who care about the issues facing the American people. It is in that caring and deep desire to help the country that they allow themselves to generalize their abilities. They come to the conclusion that if only they had the power, they could make the world a better place in which to live. They have done that in the real world, and they have addressed serious issues that impacted many people.

Experience, money and name recognition are critical in getting elected. This is not new information; this is an obvious fact. Why, then, would someone invest time, money and energy into what is clearly a futile effort if you are seeing the big picture? Having ruled out some of the reasons why someone might make a presidential run — namely, that they're stupid — then there must be another reason.

Ego certainly applies to Rick Perry. There certainly is reason to believe that being the Governor of Texas can be a logical jumping-off point for the White House, especially if your name is Bush. This is not necessarily a sign of a strong ego; in fact, it may be just the opposite. It could be that their ego's strength is such that what seems like a good message is perceived as a great message — one that is marketable all the way to Washington and into the White House.

Mark Everson developed excellent skills in finance and economics, more specifically in tax structure and reform. But is it possible for him to develop a large enough political base to run for the presidency? No one will doubt that these are important skills; but is it reasonable to believe that they form enough of a base to inspire the voting public to put Everson in the White House?

It reflects a myopic view of what the American people have as their priority. This is an example of an expert on details missing the big picture, so much so that he feels he's presidential timber. In fact, it's not missing the forest for the trees. It's seeing one tree and generalizing that to all forests.

Mark Everson is a bright, articulate individual. He is an example of a person aware of difficulties facing America and believing his skills can address the multifaceted issues and provide lasting answers. His motivation to help is laudable; however, he overestimates his ability to address issues with the skills that he has. Everson, as an OTP, is convinced that he has tools that can and will resolve the issues we face today. As the expression says, "When you are a hammer, everything looks like a nail to you."

We need both; however, we need more than that to repair the problems and construct a more viable society.

THE QVR (THE QUIT VOICE OF REASON)
Joe Biden, Carly Fiorina, Jim Gilmore, Lindsey Graham, John Kasich, Martin O'Malley, George Pataki, Jim Webb

The problem with this category is this category. Who wants a quiet voice of reason? Moreover, in terms of electability, what do you think wins out — reason or boisterous rhetoric? "Item, qe nul soit si hardy de crier havok sur peine davoir la test coupe." "Cry havoc and let slip the dogs of war," Julius Caesar, 1601. It sometimes boils down to volume versus virtue or content versus volume.

When decibels are the criteria in logic, the QVRs can and are often overpowered and out-shouted. They are often found waiting quietly to inject their form of reason into the discussion. And in the political landscape where these individuals must grow and thrive, they are often overlooked. The Marcus of Queensberry rules don't hold in the presidential election of 2016. A big mouth versus a big thought often finds this group frustrated, with a longing for the opportunity to inject their position as they are deluged by words that seem to them to have a low thought-per- word ratio. Sometimes timing and good breeding make them seem unprepared to thrust their views into the arena for consideration.

In a debate format, the QVR is not as exciting to the television reporters as is the loudmouth making a quick remark which does not respect the protocol of the debate. These are the people that make "good television." The bully and a braggart beat out the more sane and sedate in a large field of contenders.

It's almost laughable to think of Carly Fiorina in a shouting match with Donald Trump. Or an experienced debater like Joe Biden going toe-to-toe and out-shouting Chris Christie.

These are just simply two different strategies when it comes to explaining a position and trying to influence the thinking of others. In no way does this imply that the approach on the part of the QVRs reflects powerlessness, intimidation or an unwillingness to engage.

It is the difference between a battleship and a modern submarine. Those who choose the battleship strategy to engage the Quiet Voice of Reason types, would do well to remember that the last American battleship, the USS Missouri, was decommissioned for the last time in 1992.

The modern American navy of 2016 has 70 nuclear submarines. Any one is hundreds of times more powerful by itself than all battleships ever built combined. They move undetected in the world's oceans. They are much less conspicuous than the old, decommissioned battleships. Their fighting days are long passed, with the exception of the Sunday crowds that flock to visit these monuments to a less effective strategy.

For some, it's the experience, the adventure, or the fantasy. For others, it is an obsession more about winning than style or approach. It's the intra-psychic makeup of the individual that determines the category to which they belong. It is not the content of the message but the way it's delivered. And that is the unconscious structure.

The QVRs such as John Kasich, with his gentlemanly reasoned and non-confrontational strategies would certainly be a good listener in these times when knowledge is reduced to cliché and genuine insights are as rare as respect across the isles.

Be it John Kasich or the likes of Jim Webb, George Pataki, or Jim Gilmore their chances are slim and basically none of getting the nomination of their party. The reason is simple. Punch and passion payoff with both, viewers, voters and those who are wishing to back a winner. It makes no difference whether you're a Democrat or Republican, the volume of your voice and the party-line rhetoric spoken in a headline-grabbing way and on television is the end to the QVRs everywhere.

Lindsey Graham and Martin O'Malley have more in common, even though one is a Republican and the other a Democrat, than they do with a Hillary Clinton or Rand Paul. Our unconscious makeup is a critical factor in how we deal with difference. For some their first reaction is to fight, while others prefer to reflect and strategize before responding.

CHAPTER 32

OVERVIEW OF THE CANDIDATES AND CATEGORIES

The NO (Noblesse Oblige)
America's political dynasty "logical succession"

- Jeb Bush
- Lincoln Chafee
- Hillary Clinton
- Rand Paul

The M&M (Messianic Messenger)
Divine guidance in search of a miracle

- Ben Carson
- Mike Huckabee

3"F" (Fantasies – Frustration – Fury)
Passionate, angry, black-and-white thinkers

- Bob Ehrlich
- Bobby Jindal
- Mark Rubio
- Bernie Sanders
- Rick Santorum
- Scott Walker

The PP (Power Players)
Wit and will meet silver tongues and quick-thinking

- Hillary Clinton (also NO)
- Chris Christie
- Peter King
- Donald Trump

The OTP
The One Trick Pony looking for a long ride

- Mark Everson
- Rick Perry (first to drop out)

The QVR (The Quit Voice of Reason)
The submarine versus the battleship

- Joe Biden
- Carly Fiorina
- Jim Gilmore
- Lindsey Graham
- John Kasich
- Martin O'Malley
- George Pataki
- Jim Webb

CHAPTER 33

PERSONALITY TYPES
CANDIDATES AT A GLANCE

Type 1.2 The Plotter

Type 2   The Doer

Type 2.0 The Prevailer

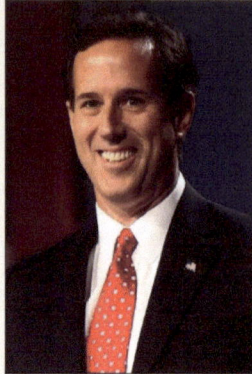

Type 2.1 The Thinker

Type 2.3 The Pouncer

Type 3 The Doubter

Type 3.0 The Determinator

Type 3.1 The Analyst

Type 3.2 The Inquisitor

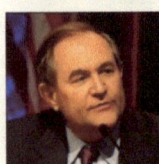

NAME	CHAPTER	PERSONALITY	NO.	ONE LINERS
Joe Biden	4	Inquisitor	3.2	*A loved politician who shoots from his lip and often misses his target.*
Jeb Bush	5	Doer	2	*A clear-thinking, nice, reasonable passionless person lacking luster.*
Ben Carson	6	Doubter	3	*Like most surgeons, sometimes wrong but never in doubt.*
Lincoln Chafee	7	Determinator	3.0	*An independent thinker, whose thinking is sometimes doubtful.*
Chris Christie	8	Inquisitor	3.2	*A scrapping Jersey boy ready to fight his way to the White House.*
Hillary Clinton	9	Pouncer	2.3	*A person who's been around for years still yelling "I'm new!"*
Ted Cruz	10	Inquisitor	3.2	*A "devoted divider" more interested in his views then uniting principles.*

Bob Ehrlich	11	Pouncer	2.3	*A bright governor with no name recognition - Bob who?*
Mark Everson	12	Doer	2	*A former big-time taxman trying to go straight in Washington.*
Carly Fiorina	13	Doer	2	*A sophisticated powerhouse with outstanding talents and abilities.*
Jim Gilmore	14	Inquisitor	3.2	*An honest fighter who won't get a "title shot" due to his lackluster demeanor.*
Lindsey Graham	15	Doubter	3	*A pro-military senator interested in bipartisan straight talk.*
Mike Huckabee	16	Doer	2	*A talented down-homeboy with the big uptown ideas.*
Bobby Jindal	17	Doer	2	*Eastern roots, Southern charm, a smart man with a plan.*
John Kasich	18	Doubter	3	*He's not charismatic, but, an informed nice guy who knows D.C. politics.*

Peter King	19	Inquisitor	3.2	*A NYC street-fighter. A pained person promising programs for D.C.*
Martin O'Malle y	20	Prevailer	2.0	*A JFK impersonator longing to re-create "Camelot" in 2016.*
George Pataki	21	Plotter	1.2	*A tired war-horse never willing to quit, always trying to be relevant.*
Rand Paul	22	Analyst	3.1	*An eye doctor with a myopic view when he looks toward Washington.*
Rick Perry	23	Plotter	1.2	*Even looking through new glasses – his boots still look dull.*
Marco Rubio	24	Doubter	3	*A meticulously grown brain hitched to one of the fastest tongues in the race.*
Bernie Sanders	25	Doubter	3	*A person who's as far left as can be and still be called a Democrat.*

Rick Santorum	26	Thinker	2.1	*A bright, serious man, needing a major humor transplant.*
Donald Trump	27	Pouncer	2.3	*A "Wild Hair" in the Republican caucus.*
Scott Walker	28	Doubter	3	*A top mid-level executive dreaming of becoming the Chief Executive.*
Jim Webb	29	Doer	2	*A genuine combat hero showing anxiety in his White House battle.*

APPENDIX 1

DEFINITIONS OF TERMS

CER Calculated Emotional Response

CSR Calculated Seductive Response

Definition of Report Level: Any behavior that is observable and testable. It is a fact.

Impact see SL1

Meta-level being here and now

NVL Non-Verbal Leak is an unconscious, repetitive, patterned movement from the shoulder up, and reflects an old decision or strategy from the past

Report Level observations what literally can be seen (first impression)

Symbolic Level of Response observable behavior that is translated to a psychological level in terms of three factors:

SL 1 THE IMPACT
How the person first perceives an event. It is real in the eyes of the person who experienced it. This shock to the system can be recorded on both levels of consciousness. Moreover, it can impact upon the person on an intra-psychic, psycho-physiological or interpersonal level as well.

SL 2 THE PRIMARY EMOTION
The basic emotion wanted to be expressed. What the person intuitively wants to do.

SL 3 THE PRIMARY COPING STRATEGY
What a person actually *does*, not necessarily the way he wants to do.

REFERENCES

ABC, BBC, CBS, CNN, FOX, NBC Television Network and their websites
Demographic details used to described the candidate's background

Associated Press website
Demographic details used to described the candidate's background

Caesar, Julius: *Cry havoc and let slip the dogs of war.* 1601

Carson, Ben: *Think big: unleashing your potential for excellence.*1996

Dalberg-Acton, John Emerich Edward: *Power tends to corrupt, and absolute power corrupts absolutely. Great men are almost always bad men.*1887

Freud, Sigmund: *Fragment of an Analysis of a Case of Hysteria.*1905

Creativecommons.org

Goodfield, Barry Austin: *Insight & Action: The role of the unconscious in crisis from the personal to international levels.* University of Westminster Press, London 1999

Goodfield, Barry Austin: *Process for Diagnosing and Treating a Psychological Condition or Assigning a Personality Classification to an Individual. Twelve Goodfield Personalities Types.*
United States Patent Application no. 12/124,938

Goodfield, Barry Austin: *Process for treating psychophysiological condition Inventor(s).* US3991744 Serial No. 570403, Filed 19750422, Issued 19761116

Goodfield, Barry Austin: *Minding Milosevic's Mind.* Forensic Examiner Summer 2006

Goodfield, Barry Austin: *Saddam Hussein: The Unconscious Mind of the Butcher of Baghdad.*
Forensic Examiner Summer 2007

Kavanaugh, James: *There Are Men Too Gentle to Live Among Wolves* 1970

Kzirkel, K.C.: Picture of Governor L. Chafee Wikimedia Commons

Lincoln, Abraham: *Nearly all men can stand adversity, but if you want to test a man's character, give him power.*

Lippenholz, Richard: Picture of Senator B.Ehrlich

Martin, George R.R.: *A Clash of Kings* 1998

McCollester, Darren: Getty Images picture of Governor J. Gilmore

Movie Mr. Smith Goes to Washington 1939

Movie Network: *I'mad as hell and I'm not going to take it anymore.*1976

Movie Patton: *Americans love a winner and will not tolerate a loser. The thought of losing is hateful to all Americans.* 1970

Movie Terminator 2: Judgement Day *Hasta la vista, baby.* 1991

New York Times, *Red Cross Dismisses President, Citing Relationship.* 11/27/2007

New York Times website: Demographic details used to described the candidates' background

Random House: Picture of cover book Carly Fiorina

Revis, Beth: *Across the Universe.* 2011

Skidmore, Gage: Photos Courtesy of

Vadon, Michael: Picture of Governor C. Christie Wikipedia Commons

Websites of all presidential candidates

Wikimedia Commons

Wikipedia, the free encyclopedia

ABOUT THE AUTHOR

Prof. Barry Austin Goodfield, Ph.D., DABFM*

Prof. Goodfield is Founding Director of The Goodfield Institute LLC in Arizona, and The Netherlands. He holds a Ph.D. in Psychology and Human Behavior. In 1996 he became President & CEO of The Goodfield Foundation: for the Study of Conflict Communication and Peace Building. In 2010 he became President & CEO of The Goodfield Media Group International LLC. In 2015 he became Founder/Director of Operation New Outlook, using the Goodfield Method to remove Post Traumatic Stress and enhance quality of life of veterans.

Dr. Barry Goodfield is a Certified Marriage and Family Therapist. He has assisted individual clients and families for more than 30 years with their issues and concerns. Dr. Goodfield specializes in identifying the unconscious nonverbal signals known as Non-Verbal Leak. His work is based on an unique patented psychotherapeutic process, which he developed in the 1970s. He holds one U.S. patent and one pending on his psychotherapeutic process. Dr. Goodfield has shared his methods with psychiatrists, psychologists, senior corporate executives, attorneys, cabinet-level officials, law enforcement and individuals around the globe.

He is a lecturer on a wide range of subjects. He appears regularly on television and radio in America and Europe. He is also an author, having published *Insight and Action: The Role of the Unconscious in Crisis from Personal to International Levels* (1999), *So You Want To Be My President?* (2011), *Relationships: A Survival Guide* vol.1 (2012), *Real Love: A Survival Guide* vol. 2 (2015).

Various international bodies such as the United Nations (International

Criminal Tribunal for the former Yugoslavia), and NATO H.Q. Brussels, as well as governments such as the former Soviet Union, The Netherlands, Lithuania, Uzbekistan, Sri Lanka, Sultanate of Oman, Ukraine, Austria and corporations have utilized the services and methodology of the Goodfield Institute and Goodfield Foundation.

For five years Dr. Goodfield was a protégé to semantics expert and United States Senator S. I. Hayakawa. He completed his Ph.D. in Psychology and Human Behavior at United States International University, with prior doctoral study at University of California Berkeley and Rutgers University.

Dr. Goodfield is a member of a number of organizations and associations including:

Diplomate, American Board of Forensic Examiners
Diplomate, American Board of Forensic Medicine*
Diplomate, American Board of Psychology Specialists, Clinical Psychology
Diplomate, American Academy of Experts in Traumatic Stress
Diplomate, National Center for Crisis Management
Member, American Psychological Association
Member, American Federation of Television and Radio Artists
Member, California Association of Marriage and Family Therapists
Member, Counter Animal and Human Trafficking Team
Member, International Society of Police Surgeons, Inc.
Member, Parliamentarians Network for Conflict Prevention
Member, Phoenix Committee on Foreign Relations
Member, SAG-AFTRA American Federation of Television and Radio Artists

Websites:
goodfieldinstitute.com
goodfieldinstituut.nl
goodfieldmediagroup.com
operationnewoutlook.com

www.ingramcontent.com/pod-product-compliance
Lightning Source LLC
Chambersburg PA
CBHW040124270326
41926CB00001B/8